A CELTIC
BOOK
OF DAYS

A CELTIC
BOOK
OF DAYS

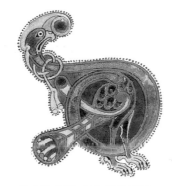

SARAH COSTLEY
AND CHARLES KIGHTLY

with 219 illustrations

THAMES AND HUDSON

Grateful acknowledgment is made for permission to use extracts from the following:
Tom Peete Cross and Clark Harris Slover, *Ancient Irish Tales*, Copyright 1936, © 1964 by Henry Holt and Company, Inc. Reprinted by permission of Henry Holt and Company, Inc. Ulick O'Connor, *Brendan Behan*, 1970, Penguin Books Ltd. Louis MacNeice, *Collected Poems*, 1979, Faber and Faber Ltd. Kenneth Hurlstone Jackson, *Early Celtic Nature Poetry*, 1935, Cambridge University Press. Gerard Murphy (ed.), *Early Irish Lyrics*, 1956, by permission of Oxford University Press. Sir James Frazer, *The Golden Bough*, by permission of A. P. Watt Ltd on behalf of Trinity College, Cambridge. Gerald of Wales, *The History and Topography of Ireland*, Penguin Books Ltd, by kind permission of the translator, John O'Meara. Mary Lavin, *In the Middle of the Fields*, from *Selected Stories*, 1964, Constable Publishers and Houghton Mifflin Co. W. B. Yeats, *Irish Fairy and Folk Tales*, and *The Collected Poems of W. B. Yeats*, by permission of A. P. Watt Ltd on behalf of Michael Yeats. Reprinted with the permission of Simon & Schuster from *Fairy & Folk Tales of Ireland*, edited by W. B. Yeats. Copyright © 1973 by Colin Smythe Ltd. Reprinted with the permission of

Scribner, A Division of Simon & Schuster from *The Collected Works of W. B. Yeats*, Volume I: *The Poems*, revised and edited by Richard J. Finneran. Copyright © 1983, 1989 by Anne Yeats. Gwyn Jones and Thomas Jones (translators), *The Mabinogion*, 1949, J. M. Dent. Dylan Thomas, *The Poems of Dylan Thomas*, David Higham Associates Ltd on behalf of J. M. Dent. 'A Refusal to Mourn the Death, by Fire, of a Child in London', from *The Poems of Dylan Thomas*. Copyright © 1945 by The Trustees for the Copyrights of Dylan Thomas. Reprinted by permission of New Directions Publishing Corp. James Joyce, *A Portrait of the Artist as a Young Man* © The Estate of James Joyce. Padraic Fiacc, *Ruined Pages*, 1994, The Blackstaff Press Ltd. Maud Gonne MacBride, *A Servant of the Queen*, Colin Smythe Ltd, Publishers. Somerville and Ross, *Some Experiences of an Irish R. M.*, Copyright E. OE. Somerville and Martin Ross, reproduced by permission of Curtis Brown Ltd, London. Somerville and Ross, *Some Experiences of an Irish R. M.*, Little, Brown and Company (UK).

Every effort has been made to trace the copyright holders of material quoted, and any omissions are regretted.

Foreword

The Celts

Who are the Celts? A definition has its difficulties: myths about the Celtic character are so strong that it is sometimes hard to see the subtleties and complexities for the broad strokes. The roll call of larger-than-life personalities, warriors, literary heroes and geniuses of imagination, invention and humour is seemingly endless.

Classical commentators described the Celts as a tall, fair-complexioned and large-limbed people, although Tacitus noted that the people of southern Wales were small and swarthy, with dark, curly hair; he found them fiery of temper, courageous to the point of foolhardiness and fond of good wit. Whoever they actually were, and modern commentators prefer to think of these Celts of prehistory as a shifting tide of tribes with a distinct culture rather than as a racial group, they came to dominate much of central and western Europe in the millennium before Christ, arriving in the Highlands of Scotland and the Western Isles, Ireland, Wales, the Isle of Man, north-western France and Cornwall.

Much in the early descriptions seems to have been accurate: the Celts were warlike; they valued their bards and their druids; they wore flowing hairstyles and golden torques, pins and brooches and rode in chariots (23 October); they were boastful – just as the ancient Irish tales of Iron Age society featuring Cú Chullain (6 August), the Ulster heroes of the Red Branch, and archaeological excavations have shown.

They were certainly brave. Though Asterix, Obelix and Getafix the Gauls are fictional, their mortal counterparts caused Caesar a great deal of trouble in Brittany before he crushed them in *c*. AD 60 by employing the might of the Roman Empire. Boudicca, the Amazon in her chariot; Brian Boru; Owen Glendower; William Wallace; and Robert the Bruce: all these are Celts known for their courage against impossible odds. And as for the regard in which their bards were held, William McGonagall (8 January) could tell a tale.

Eoin Mac Néill, the Irish scholar and revolutionary, in his *Phases of Irish History* (1919), described the prehistoric Celts, rulers for a time of swathes of Europe and pillagers of Rome, thus: '[They] were perhaps the most intensely proud class of men that ever existed.' Pride was their one, fatal, defect.

This book is a celebration of Celtic courage, wit, resourcefulness, scholarship and brilliance. But it is also an attempt to rescue the good name of the Celts from over-simplification. Pride, for example, as an alleged defect may be belied by at least some of the saints and sceptics who figure here: one could hardly call the delightful Saints Kentigern and Corentin arrogant (14 January and 12 December), and the Breton peasant who instructed Saint Peter did so with commendable simplicity (20 October). The sensitivity and kindness of Fionn Mac Cumhal, too, shows great humility in a renowned and high-ranking warrior – no vainglorious chieftain he. Attentive to the needs of the weak, he loved animals (18 April), and had an intimate understanding of nature (16 November). This appreciation of the natural world is evident in the earliest to the most recent poetry of the Gael and Gaul – witness the sixth-century poet Taliesin whose 'Pleasant Things' are sketched on the page for 28 September, the eighteenth-century Cathal Buidhe Mac Giolla Ghunna's lament for the lonely bittern (9 March), and the wealth of medical tracts advising on natural – if sometimes peculiar – cures.

The Celtic genius shows up well among orators – on 27 October, an intrepid Welshman shows the legendary Christian ruler Prester John what's what and who's who – and among travellers and explorers. Early Celtic saints, whether on pilgrimage, essaying the conversion of the heathen British and Europeans, or in pursuit of peace on an isolated rock in the ocean, boarded their coracles and millstones and sailed for distant lands, following as if by instinct the bow-waves of their pre-Christian ancestors. They probably discovered America – if the stories of Saint Brendan (16 May) and Prince Madawg (12 October) are to be believed – long before anyone else. Sir Ernest Shackleton (15 February: if not strictly Celtic, he was at least born in Ireland), and Mungo Park from Selkirkshire (2 December) show just that mixture of breathtaking courage and endurance that their predecessors had possessed in such impressive quantities.

Language – Brythonic/British (P-Celtic) of the Welsh, Cornish and Bretons, and the Goidelic/Gallic (Q-Celtic) of Ireland, Scotland and the Isle of Man –

defines and unites the Celts in this book. These languages have long lived in the shadow of the French and English tongues, but despite all difficulties and unequal competition they will not be given up. Cornish and Manx, long ago declared dead, are still fiercely contended, while Welsh, Irish and Breton are small-language success stories.

Honoré de Balzac, in his *The Chouans* (26 July), wrote: 'Today, in 1829, a newspaper remarks that a Breton regiment of the French Army has arrived back in Nantes after travelling across France and being garrisoned in Spain, without a single man having learned a word of French or Spanish. It was Brittany on the move, traversing France like a Gallic tribe.'

Scots, Bretons, Irish and Welsh can be found in every part of the globe, still firmly attached to their own culture and language. They celebrate Burns Night in Peru, St Patrick's Day in Brooklyn, and speak Welsh in Patagonia and Scottish Gaelic on Prince Edward Island.

No limit has been placed on the Celtic sources for the book, which consequently spans a good 2,500 years. To Celts, part-Celts, and those with Celtic sympathies, this book is dedicated.

The Celtic Year

As the Celts counted time by the number of nights, rather than days (see Julius Caesar's comment on 11 April), so the Celtic year began on 1 November, at Samhain, summer's end, when the darkness began. On 1 May, Beltane, the second, light half of the year was entered. Between these festivals came another, Lughnasa, the feast of the god Lugh, on 1 August, and, in some places at least, Imbolg, the feast of lambs and milking ewes, punctuated the dark half of the cycle on 1 February.

Samhain is associated with death, as are the Christian feasts of All Saints and All Souls (1 and 2 November respectively); Imbolg or oimelc is echoed down the ages by the Christian feast of St Brigid, herself of pagan origin. Beltane, fire of the immortal Bél or Belenus, who seems to have been a solar god, is still an important festival of renewal. Lughnasa is and always was to do with the beginning of harvest, of course, and with sports and games and fairs – the holiday season.

The New Style and Old Style dates referred to in the text are the result of an emendation to the calendar of Julius Caesar, which had been followed by Europeans from 45 BC. Changes were made by astronomers in the late sixteenth century on the orders of Pope Gregory XIII in 1582 and adopted in Catholic Europe shortly afterwards; these changes only reached Britain in 1752, when eleven days in September were ordered to be omitted.

JANUARY

cold air month

Breton: *Genver*   Cornish: *Genvar*
Irish: *Eanáir, Gionbhar*   Manx: *Jerrey Geuree*
Scottish: *Gionbhar*   Welsh: *Ionawr*

1
New Year's Day, New Style: begin the year with hard, invigorating exercise

'On New Year's Day a game of football or shinty was played in the Highlands by one parish against the next, and no confines of pitch were observed. The match would begin at the parish bounds and continue into darkness or a free fight.'

Sir Eneas Mackintosh of Mackintosh, *Notes*, 1774–83

Some call January *an mios marbh*, 'the dead month', some December, while some apply *na tri miosa marbh, an raithe marbh,* 'the dead quarter', and *raithe marbh na bliadhna* to the winter months when nature is asleep.

'Matrimony is avoided in the month of January, which is called in the Erse the "cold month".'

Thomas Pennant, *A Tour in Scotland and Voyage to the Hebrides*, 1772

2
In the Christmas season do not forget to share your feast with the wild birds and beasts, unprotected from the cold and darkness

Cernunnos, the horned god, lord of the animals
'I asked him what power he had over the animals. "I will show thee, little man," said he. And he took the club in his hand, and with it struck a stag a mighty blow till it gave out a mighty belling, and in answer to its belling wild animals came till they were as numerous as the stars in the firmament, so that there was scant room for me to stand in the clearing with them and all those serpents and lions and vipers and all kinds of animals. And he looked on them and bade them go graze. And they bowed their heads, and did him obeisance, even as humble subjects would do to their lord.'

The Lady of the Fountain, Arthurian tale, medieval Welsh translated by G. and T. Jones

Midwinter, Old Style: keep the Yule fires burning

'The Fire Festivals of Beltane, Halloween, Midsummer and Yule had this in common – they were all purificatory, designed to purge air and earth and sky of unclean and hostile influences. They thus paved the way for prosperity by land and sea. Two forms of fire appear. There is the stationary bonfire, sometimes as at Beltane the source from which the torches are lit, sometimes as at Burghead the culmination of the fire celebrations. Besides the static fire, there is the portable fire, carried by lighted torches, "Clavies" around the corn, the fields, the flocks, the herds, the houses and the boats. In later times, at least, witches are the enemy against whom the sacred fire is directed.'

J. M. McPherson, *Primitive Beliefs in the North East of Scotland*, 1929

Sailors may have had more to fear than bad weather

Witches could raise the wind, and calm it down again. These powers were so useful to sailors that the Isle of Man witches sold knotted cords to ships' masters. When the first knot was untied a good wind sprang up, the second knot raised a stronger wind, the third a gale. Further south on the Atlantic seaboard, according to the first-century AD Roman geographer Pomponius Mela, nine priestesses called the Gallizenae lived under vows of chastity on the Ile de Sein where they raised storms, told fortunes to passing sailors, and turned themselves into animal shapes at will.

'They reached the Land of Women. Their leader called to Bran from the shore, "Come here, Bran son of Febal, you are welcome." Bran did not dare to go to land. The woman threw a ball of thread to Bran, and he caught it in his hand, where it stuck fast. The woman pulled the coracle into the port by the thread, and he stayed there many years.'

The Voyage of Bran, Irish, eighth century

Christmas Eve, Old Style

Highland Weather Almanack

'The highlanders form a sort of almanack or presage of the weather for the ensuing year in the following manner. They make observation on twelve days, beginning at the last of December, and hold as an infallible rule that whatsoever weather happens on each of those days, the same will prove to agree in the correspondent months. Thus, January is to answer to the weather of December the 31st, February to that of January 1st; and so with the rest. Old people still pay great attention to this augury.'

Thomas Pennant, *A Tour in Scotland and Voyage to the Hebrides*, 1772

Old Christmas was observed in the Highlands on what is now known as Twelfth Night

In the Celtic lands of Britain, as in England, the people did not at first take kindly to the introduction of the New Style calendar in 1752, and tenaciously clung to the old order of things, including the stubborn conviction that 6 January was the 'real' Christmas day.

'From Twelfth Day, the days begin to lengthen by a cock's span or stride.'
Breton proverb

The Feast of the Epiphany, Little Christmas Day, is also called *coir-ceim-coilleach* or 'the cocks step', the first noticeable lengthening of the daylight hours. In the Christian Calendar it is the day when the manifestation of Christ to the wise men of the east is celebrated.

'The Epiphany is *Gwyl Ystwyll,* or *Yr Ystwyll. Ystwyll* is simply the Latin *stella*, but being an uncommon word it is explained in the Welsh Prayer Book by the alternative title *Seren wyl*, "Star Festival". The name *Festum Stella* was peculiar to the Celtic Church.'

Revd John Fisher, *The Welsh Calendar*, 1895

Bring a spray of the Holy Thorn (the root-stock is in Glastonbury) into the house and it will bloom today in honour of the Saviour's birth

'On the day after Twelfth Day, in East Cornwall, all Christmas greenery comes down. Beware, however, of burning it, for this would be unlucky.'

T. Quiller Couch, *Western Antiquary*, 1883

Holly (*Celyn,* Welsh; *Cuileann,* Irish; *Ilex aquifolium,* Latin) is a symbol of hope in midwinter. It is the tree of the oak-god's brother – or father – the Green Knight or holly-god, who presided over the sleeping half of the year. Paleobotany has shown that holly, with other small trees such as the whitethorn, the rowan and the elderberry, became widespread as secondary growth after forest clearance by early farmers. The reverence in which holly was held may be due to the fact that the wood was traditionally used as the peg or 'crook stick' from which a pot was hung over the fire, symbol of light and life.

The first Monday after Twelfth Day, was called in Welsh *Dydd Gwyl Geiliau*, 'The Festival of the Sheepfolds'

'There is a Gwent saying: "*Dydd gwyl Geiliau, at y bara haidd a'r bacsau*", "Plough Monday, resume ordinary fare and working clothing."'

Revd John Fisher, *The Welsh Calendar*, 1895

An incident in the life of a working poet

'During the holiday week of the New-year I was taken to a public house by a party of my friends and admirers, and requested to give them an entertainment, for which I was to be remunerated by them.

Of course, you ought to know that while singing a good song, or giving a good recitation, it helps to arrest the company's attention from the drink; yes! in many cases it does, my friends. Such, at least was the case with me – at least the publican thought so – for – what do you think? – he devised a plan to bring my entertainment to an end abruptly, and the plan was, he told the waiter to throw a wet towel at me.'

William McGonagall, *Reminiscences*, 1890

**Owls may be active now,
hooting and shrieking eerily**

Blodeuwedd, 'flower-face', a woman magically
made of flowers to be the wife of Llew Llaw Gyffes,
fell in love with Gronw Pebyr and plotted with him to
be rid of her husband: as punishment Llew turned her
into a bird of darkness of which all others are afraid.

But Llew was invulnerable, and Blodeuwedd had to find out how he could be slain
not an easy death to contrive: he had to stand with one foot on a dead stag and the oth
cauldron which was used as a bath and thatched with a roof, and be killed with a spea
had taken a year to make.

Fourth Branch of the *Mabinogion*, Welsh, eleventh century, edited by G. and T. Jones

Scurvy grass, *Môrlwyau Meddygol* (medicinal sea-spoons)

In Irish, *Biolar Trá*, 'cress of the strand', it is abundant on cliffs and sea shores,
whether marshy or rocky. The whole plant should be crushed in vinegar to make a
lotion for mouth ulcers. It is best known, however, as a protection against scurvy, as
it is rich in vitamin C; sailors collected it whenever they found it and ate it as a cure.

The Adventures of Teigue, son of Cian

'With victuals and stores they filled their currach so that, though they kept the sea
for a whole year, they had so much as would keep them of meat and drink, and of
right good raiment.'

Book of Lismore, Irish, fifteenth century

Hogmanay, Old Style, when it is wiser to stay indoors, safe from fairy activities

'On Twelve Eve in Christmas, they used to set up as high as they can a sieve of oats, and in it a dozen candles set round, and in the centre one larger, all lighted. This in memory of our Saviour and His Apostles, lights of the world.'

Sir Henry Piers, *Description of the County of West Meath*, 1682

'In the west of Ireland on the eve of Twelfth Night the "Christmas Loaf" was banged against the doors and windows of the house to warn away famine.'

Journal of the Royal Society of Antiquaries of Ireland, 1853

New Year's Day, Old Style

'The birds of the world, power without ill, it is to welcome the sun at the nones of January whatever the hour that their flock calls from the dark wood.'

Durham Cathedral Library, Hunter MS 100

In the early years of the twentieth century, St Kildans still used the Old Style calendar and celebrated New Year on this day. In the Irish calendar, New Year's Day has come to assume some of the auguries proper to the old New Year of Samhain, the first of November. The luck and prosperity of the whole household, for example, is foretold by what happens – or is made to happen – on this day.

'To eat millet and herring on New Year's Day ensures easy circumstances for the year.'

Manx saying

January

Handsel Monday falls about now

The minister of Tillicoultry reports: 'William Hunter, a collier, was cured in the year 1758 of an inveterate rheumatism or gout, by drinking freely of new ale. The poor man had been confined to his bed for a year and a half, having almost entirely lost the use of his limbs. On the evening of Handsel Monday (i.e. the first Monday of the New Year, Old Style) some of his neighbours came to make merry with him. Though he could not rise, yet he always took his share of ale, as it passed round the company, and, in the end, became much intoxicated. The consequence was that he had the use of his limbs next morning, and was able to walk about. He lived more than twenty years after this, and never had the smallest return of his old complaint.'
John Brand, *A Statistical Account of Scotland*, 1793

'You shouldn't pay your debts on Handsel Monday or you'll be paying them all year round.'
Wicklow saying

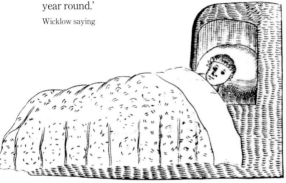

Festival of St Kentigern, first bishop of Glasgow (died AD 603), to whom as a baby St Serf gave the name Mungo, or Darling

The wife of King Rydderch foolishly gave her husband's ring to a favourite. He, seeing it on the finger of the sleeping knight, removed it stealthily and threw it into the sea. When he asked his queen to produce the ring she appealed to St Kentigern for help, and he despatched one of his monks to catch the salmon who had swallowed the ring. The saint's kindness is commemorated on the arms of the city of Glasgow.

Winter storm

'The ocean is full, the sea is in
flood, lovely is the home of ships;
the sandy wind has made eddies
around Inbher na da Ainmhech;
the rudder is swift upon the
wide sea.

It is not peaceful, a wild
troubled sleep, with feverish
triumph, with furious strife; the
swan's hue covers them, the plain
full of sea-beasts and its denizens; the hair of the wife of Manannan is tossed about.

The wave with mighty fury has fallen across each wide dark river-mouth; wind
has come, winter's fury has slain us, around Kintyre, round the land of Scotland; the
flooded torrent gushes forth, mountainous and raging.

Son of God the Father of vast hosts, protect me from the horror of wild tempests!
Righteous Lord of the Feast, only protect me from the mighty blast, from Hell with
towering tempest.'

Irish, eleventh century

Treat ailments concomitant with the Festive Season

'If a man vomit excessively, let him immerse his testicles in vinegar. It will cure him.'
'If a man be irritable of mind, let him drink celery juice frequently: it will relieve his
mood, and produce joy.'
'From the condition of a man's urine, may be distinguished his defects, dangers,
fears and diseases, whether he be present or absent: if the colour be yellow-gold it
shows that food and drink are perfectly digested in the stomach. If deep, liver-
coloured red, or greenish, it shows that food is properly digested in the stomach. If
black, or of a leaden hue, or milky, the food is not being digested in the stomach.'
Meddygon Myddfai, Welsh, thirteenth century

17 A good day to trim wicks

'The month of January, the valley is
    smoky,
The cup-bearer is weary, the wandering
    bard is in distress,
The raven is thin, the hum of bees is rare,
The byre is empty, the kiln is cold;
Degraded is the man who is not worthy to
    be asked for anything;
Woe to him who loves his three enemies
Cynfelan spoke truth
"The best candle for man is good sense."'

Welsh, *c.* fifteenth century, translated by K. H. Jackson

18 The Merrow (*Móruadh*, Irish; *Morvenna*, Welsh), the maiden of the sea, is not uncommon on the wilder coasts

'The male Merrows (if you can use
such a phrase – I have never heard
the masculine of Merrow) have
green teeth, green hair, pig's eyes
and red noses; but their women are
beautiful, for all their fish tails and
the little duck-like scale between
their fingers.'

W. B. Yeats (1865–1939), *Irish Fairy and Folk Tales*

A Cornish mermaid is carved on a
pew-end in Zennor church. She is
said to have attended services
generation after generation, until, in
the fifteenth century, she fell in love
with the voice of the churchwarden's
son and took him to live with her
below the waves of Pendower Cove.

Porridge and toast makes a good winter breakfast

In Skye 'the diet generally used consists of fresh food, for they seldom taste any that is salted, except butter. The generality eat but little flesh, and only persons of distinction eat it every day and make three meals, for the rest eat only two, and they eat more boiled than roasted. Their ordinary diet is butter, cheese, milk, potatoes, colworts, brochan, i.e. oatmeal and water boiled. The latter taken with some bread is the constant food of several thousands of both sexes in this and other isles, during the winter and spring; yet they undergo many fatigues both by land and sea, and are very healthful . . . '

Martin Martin, *A Description of the Western Islands of Scotland*, 1703

Waulking, or shrinking, a cloth taken from the loom was a Highlands occupation of the winter months

Sew the ends of the cloth together to form a circle, soak it in hot urine and place it on a trestle table around which an even number of women are sitting. The cloth is then to be passed sunwise between them, kneaded with the hands all the while, to the rhythm of a song such as this:

'I'll not go to a man without a boat,
I prefer a man of quiet conversation
I'll not go to a man without a boat

I'll not go to the carpenter who works with pine
He'll leave me black with tar

I'll not go to the blacksmith's son
Though he would mend the tongs

I'll never go to anyone
Except the man who already asked me

I will get quiet sleep
If I don't stay on the boat tonight.'

Donald MacCormick, *Hebridean Folksongs*, 1893

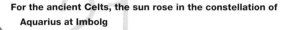

For the ancient Celts, the sun rose in the constellation of Aquarius at Imbolg

In Aquarius the sick man shall come into danger of his life and his bladder and genitals suffer most: those who shall be born are likely to live and the bladder suffers.

Apostle: Matthew

Ruler: Crius

Medieval Irish Zodiac, Basle Library

'Concerning the treatment of Hiccup: which is treated both generally and specially. Generally: as by sneezing, by prolonged sleep, by holding the breath; and by friction of the extremities, and by tales of horror.'

Medical tract, Irish, fifteenth century, B.L. Harleian 546

William Paterson, financier, original projector of the Bank of England and promoter of a scheme for establishing a new colony at Darien, on the Panama Isthmus, was born this day in 1655 (or 1658) at Tinwald, Dumfriesshire

The Scottish Parliament created the Company of Scotland to finance the project and the whole nation backed it – the English did not. On 26 July 1698 the fleet of five ships, the *Caledonia*, *St Andrew*, *Unicorn*, *Dolphin* and *Endeavour* sailed from Leith with 1,200 men.

The whole sailed amid the praises, the prayers and the tears of relations, friends and countrymen; 'and neighbouring nations', says Sir Hugh Dalrymple, Lord-president, 'saw with a mixture of surprise and respect the poorest nation in Europe sending forth the most gallant colony which had ever gone forth from the old world to the new world'.

Unable to obtain supplies because of English opposition, the young colony soon ran into trouble, compounded by the attacks of Spanish troops. Paterson returned in 1699, his health impaired but his spirit unabated.

Chambers and Thomson, *Eminent Scotsmen*, 1870

A description of Irish monks on the Continent

'They seldom travelled otherwise in companies. They wore long flowing hair, and coloured some parts of the body, especially the eyelids. They were provided with long walking-sticks, with flasks, and with leathern wallets. They used waxed writing tablets as well as skins. It is also stated that they were expert in catching fish.'

Margaret Stokes, *Early Christian Art in Ireland*, nineteenth century

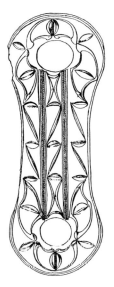

In winter take the whole sorrel plant (*samhadh*, Irish; *sealbhag*, Scottish Gaelic) and boil it up to make a red dye. Set with a little alum.

'So fond were the ancient Irish of colour that they dyed horses and pet animals to suit their taste. White horses with red ears, their long tails dyed purple, seem to have been favourites, especially with royalty. Red Conall's horses were white with crimson manes and tails.'

S. H. O'Grady, *Silva Gadelica*, 1892

St Paul's Pitcher Day: preparation for the next day's fair in Bodmin

'An old custom used to prevail on St Paul's Pitcher day, as St Paul's Eve was called in Cornwall. The tin miners would leave their work, set up a pitcher full of water, pelt it with stones until it was broken and then go to an inn, there to fill and refill a fresh pitcher with ale and pass the rest of the day in revelry ... As late as the year 1859, the boys of Bodmin used to parade the town with pitchers, which they threw into every open doorway, shouting the words "Paul's Eve and here's a heave".'

Daily Chronicle, 24 January 1906

'This shire is improperly called Flintshire there being noe flints in all the country; there are great coale putts of the Cannell Coale thats cloven huge great pieces, they have great wheeles that are turned with horses that draw up the water and so drain the Mines which would else be overflowed so as they could not dig the coale.'

The Journeys of Celia Fiennes, 1698

Eat haggis and bashed neeps with whisky: it is Burns Night

'The illustrious bard, the poet of Scotland, and not only of Scotland, but of nature at large' was born, the eldest of seven children, at Alloway, in 1759.

'But pleasures are like poppies spread
You seize the flow'r, its bloom is shed;
Or like the snow falls in the river –
A moment white, then melts for ever;
Or like the borealis race,
That flit ere you can point their place;
Or like the rainbow's lovely form
Evanishing amid the storm.
Nae man can tether time nor tide . . . '

Robert Burns (1759–1796), *Tam O'Shanter*

Also the birthday of Robert Boyle, in 1627

'The Honourable Robert Boyle, Esq., that profound Philosopher, accomplished Humanist, and excellent Divine, was borne at Lismor in the County of Corke [fourteenth child of the great earl of that county]. He was nursed by an Irish Nurse, after the Irish manner, wher they putt the child into a pendulous Satchell (insted of a Cradle) with a slitt for the Child's head to peepe out.'

John Aubrey (1626–1697), *Brief Lives*

Pass long dark winter evenings in storytelling

'Something like a stunted, blackened branch was sticking out of the peat, ending in a set of short, thickish twigs. This is what it seemed. The dogs were barking at it. It was, really, a human hand and arm, disclosed by the slipping of the bank, undermined by the brook, which was swollen by the recent rains.

The dogs were sniffing and yelping about it.
"It's a hand!", cried Wealdon, with an oath.
"A hand?" I echoed.
We were both peering at it, having drawn near, stooping and hesitating as men do in a curious horror.'

J. Sheridan LeFanu, *Wylder's Hand*, 1898

Beware the goddess of death and winter, Veiled Vera, whose powers are now at their height

'The Cailleach Beara is the third celebrated hag of Celtic folklore, found in Scotland, throughout Ireland, especially the Bear peninsula, and in the Isle of Man; she is of huge stature, the maker of mountains, islands and cairns, keeper of bitter weather.

It is narrated that on one occasion she turned Fionn MacCool into a decrepit old man, but his soldiers threatened to dig through Slieve Gullian in Armagh and drive her out of a cave in which she had her residence unless she restored Fionn to his form and symmetry.'

W. G. Wood-Martin, *Traces of the Elder Faiths of Ireland*, 1902

In the eighth century she became the subject of a monk's poem about the death of the old ways:

'I am the old Woman of Beare
An ever-new smock I used to wear:
Today – such is my mean estate –
I wear not even a cast-off smock.

It is riches
Ye love, it is not men
In the time when *we* lived
It was men we loved.'

Translated by Kuno Meyer, 1913

Month of the rowan, the wizard's tree

Even a twig of the rowan will prevent witchcraft in the house, on the farm and at sea; it will keep a corpse in its coffin and the dead in their graveyard, and protect the unwary against fascination by fairies.

'Rowan was protective rather than generative: it did not bring blessing so much as ward off evil – from whence it was thought to be the abode of a good spirit.'

J. M. McPherson, *Primitive Beliefs in the North-East of Scotland*, 1929

Ensuring the sterility of the land

'Before Candlemas we went be-east Kinloss, and there we yoked a plough of toads. The Devil held the plough, and John Young, our Officer, did drive the plough. Toads did draw the plough as oxen, couch-grass was the harness and trace-chains, a gelded animal's horn was the coulter, and a piece of gelded animal's horn was the sock.'

Isobel Gowdie, Morayshire witch, 1662, from R. Pitcairn, *Criminal Trials*

Feast day of Saint Gildas the Wise

Born to the west of Glasgow in the late fifth or early sixth century AD he visited Ireland, where his teachings had a profound influence on Irish monasticism. He spent most of his life on the Isle of Flatholm in the Bristol Channel, then moved to Brittany where he lived as a hermit on the island of Rhuys in Morbihan Bay. About AD 540 he wrote *De Excidio Britanniae*, a 'terrible indictment of the scandalous lives of his contemporaries, both ecclesiastics and laymen' which highlighted 'the miseries, the errors and the ruin of Britain'. His feast day is celebrated still in Vannes (in Carhaix his festival has assumed the character of St Swithin's and is a fateful rain-day), but nowhere in the British Isles. He died *c.* 570.

Ogmios, the Celtic god of speech and poetry, is credited with the creation of the Ogham script

This alphabet is written as strokes across or either side of a line and was much used for inscriptions on stones and weapons between about AD 300–500. Examples have been found in Ireland, particularly in the south, Wales, in the Isle of Man and in Scotland. A version has been found on some of the Western Isles. There are also one or two in western Britain, and one in southern England. Each letter corresponds to a tree or a climber (except for the reed of Samhain), and a calendar month. January's letter is L and the tree is the rowan.

Saint Brigid's Eve

The Saint of Kildare is thought to be not one but three pre-Christian goddesses, of poetry and learning, of healing, and of the craft of the smith.

'It was she who first made the whistle for calling one to another through the night.'
Lady Gregory (1859–1932), *Gods and Fighting Men*

On St Brigid's Eve a ribbon is placed on the window sill outside during the night. The ribbon is said to lengthen during the night and is ever after preserved as a cure for headache.

A cross of green rushes should be made, which will protect the house from fire and other harm for the coming year.

FEBRUARY
the whirling month

Breton: *C'houevrer*   Cornish: *Huevral*
Irish: *Feabhra, mí na ngaoth* (month of winds)   Manx: *Toshiaght Arr*
Scottish: *ceud mhios an earraich* (first month of spring)   Welsh: *Chwef.*

The Feast Day of St Brigid, 'the Mary and Juno of the Gael'. This is Imbolg, the festival of spring, of fecundity, milk and lambs

'Women made up a bed, perhaps with a sheaf of corn dressed as a woman in it, and that Bride was formally invoked and welcomed. On that day the fishermen of Barra used to cast lots for their fishing grounds.'

M. F. Shaw, *Folksongs and Folklore of South Uist*, 1955

In Uist the dandelion is called the *bearnan Bride*, the little notched of Bride; in Ireland the same name is given to the juniper. The nipplewort, with its yellow serrated flower appearing in late summer, is called bride's leaf.

Candlemas, feast of the purification of the Blessed Virgin Mary; half-way through winter

'The mother of Christ and the mother of Erin are said to be first cousins. One story has it that while Mary went to the temple forty days after giving birth to be purified Brigid created a diversion, to give her a little peace and quiet from the crowds of onlookers, by walking through the streets wearing a wooden frame on her head stuck with lighted candles.'

Kildare Archaeological Society, 1908

For good weather throughout the year today's weather should be abominable – but bright enough to lure animals out of hibernation.

'It is a loss in a land to sie a fair Candlemas day.'

'If Candlemas is fair and clear
There'll be two winters in the year.'

Scottish sayings

'To see a hedgehog on this day is a herald of good ploughing weather.'

Irish saying

February

The feast day of Saint Blaise, patron of woolcombers, wild animals, and those suffering from afflictions of the neck

An Armenian, Saint Blaise is said to have visited Britain, and to have made landfall at the Cornish town which bears his name. An effigy is preserved in the church, and in his honour, ball games are still played at St Columb Major on Shrove Tuesday.

'A simple remedy for the relief of pain in the neck: take the roots of celandines and pound them together with fennel, garlic, wine or vinegar and a little butter. Apply this as a poultice to the nape and the pain and swelling will disperse.'

Meddygon Myddfai, Welsh, thirteenth century

Eat Welsh Cakes before Lent

You will need: one pound of self-raising flour, half a pound of butter or lard, half a pound of currants, half a teaspoonful of salt, one egg, a little sugar and a cup of milk.

Mix the butter or lard and flour well together with the hands, then add the sugar and currants. Beat the egg separately, and add to it the salt and a cup of milk and pour into the dry ingredients. The mixture should be just stiff. Place an iron pan, rubbed with lard, over a fire that is not too sharp to warm. Roll out the mixture and cut into rounds. Brown the cakes in the pan on one side, then turn them over. Leave them for five minutes and they should be done.

One of the virtues of rosemary

'Put the flowers or leaves under your head in bed, and you will not be troubled with disagreeable dreams, or oppressed with anxiety of mind.'

Meddygon Myddfai, Welsh, thirteenth century

'Mountain snow, white is every place;
the raven is accustomed to sing:
good does not come of excessive sleeping.'

Welsh, tenth/eleventh centuries, translated by K. H. Jackson

'Himself [Earl Gerald] and his warriors are now sleeping in a long cavern under the Rath of Mullaghmast. There is a table running along through the middle of the cave. The Earl is sitting at the head, and his troopers down along in complete armour both sides of the table, and their heads resting on it. Their horses, saddled and bridled, are standing behind their masters in their stalls at each side; and when the day comes, the miller's son that's to be born with six fingers on each hand will blow his trumpet, and the horses will stamp and whinny, and the knights awake and mount their steeds, and go forth to battle.'

Eileen O'Faolain, *Irish Sagas and Folk Tales*, 1954

In early February unmarried girls throw stones at scald crows to discover from which direction their husbands will come. If the bird doesn't move they are destined to remain spinsters

The black-and-grey hooded or scald crow (Irish, *Feannóg*; Latin, *Corvus corone cornix*) evolved separately from the carrion crow during the last Ice Age and followed the retreating ice northward: nowadays it is a common sight in Ireland and North-West Scotland and rare elsewhere. Though it may differ from the black crow in plumage and in having more sociable habits, its reputation is no better: scald crows are the emblem of Macha, one of the three sisters who make up the Mór-ríoghanna, goddesses of battle and carnage.

'Macha's fruit-crop is the heads of those slaughtered.'

Yellow Book of Lecan, Irish, fourteenth/fifteenth centuries, edited by Whitley Stokes

The festival of Saint Appollonia, patron saint of teeth

'He who cleans his teeth with the point of his knife, may soon clean them with the haft.'

Book of Iago ab Dewi, Welsh, fourteenth century

In Wales 'both sexes take great care of their teeth, more than I have seen in any country. They are constantly cleaning them with green hazel shoots and then rubbing them with woollen cloths until they shine like ivory. To protect their teeth they never eat hot food, but only what is tepid, or slightly warm.'

Gerald of Wales, *Description of Wales*, late twelfth century

'If, by accident, you find the back tooth of a horse, carry it about with you as long as you live, and you shall never want for money; but it must be found by chance.'

Lady Wilde, *Superstitions and Cures*, 1888

Consider your nuptial prospects: Lent is approaching and no marriages may take place – on the mainland

Three Sundays before Ash Wednesday is called *Domhnach na gCogarnach*, or Whispering Sunday, as the marriage brokers begin to make arrangements among the unbetrothed of the parish. Two Sundays before Lent is known as *Domnach na mBruidearnach*, or Dunging (nudging) Sunday as the dealing becomes more desperate. The first Sunday in Lent is called *Domnach na Smuit*, or Snout Sunday for those who haven't managed to get themselves married by Shrove Tuesday.

Irish lore

The Skellig lists

The monks of Skellig Michael resisted the reformation of the church calendar, and so began and ended Lent one month later than the mainland – allowing an extra month for marriage.

'After marriage, the bride immediately walks round the church, unattended by the bridegroom. The precaution of loosening every knot about the new-joined pair is strictly observed.'

Thomas Pennant, *A Tour in Scotland and Voyage to the Hebrides*, 1772

'A man cannot thrive except his wife let him.'

Fergusson, *Scottish Proverbs*, 1641

9

The birthday of Brendan Behan, the Borstal Boy

He was born in Dublin in 1923 and died there on 20 March 1964.
In his teens Brendan joined the IRA, as was the family tradition, and was sentenced
to three years detention in Borstal for possession of explosives.
As a child Brendan was his formidable grandmother's favourite, and she would
often take him drinking with her. One night as they returned home a passer-by
remarked to her 'Isn't it terrible, ma'am, to see such a beautiful little boy deformed?'
'How dare you?' said his granny, 'He is not deformed. He's just drunk.'
Ulick O'Connor, *Brendan Behan*, 1970

Behan was an admirer of the eighteenth-century Kerry poet, labourer and
schoolmaster, Owen Roe O'Sullivan, who died in penury.

'Here's what I think of a rake's life.'

'When weakness comes and old age draws up to me,
I lack for clothing, I lose my strength,
My limbs in the morning shake and shiver,
My words are savourless and weak my voice.'

10

Lent is approaching: think about diet

'Cathal Mac Finguine was a good king, who governed Munster; a great warrior
prince was he. A warrior of this sort: with the edge of a hound, he ate like a horse.
Satan, viz. a demon of gluttony that was in his throat, used to devour his rations

with him. A pig and a cow
and a bull-calf of three hands,
with three score cakes of pure
wheat, and a vat of new ale,
and thirty heathpoult's eggs,
that was his first dole, besides
his other snack, until his
great feast was ready for him.
As regards the great feast,
that passes account or
reckoning.'

The Vision of Mac Conglinne, Irish,
fourteenth century, edited by Kuno
Meyer, 1892

February

The festival of Saint Gobnat: Oengus in his Calendar exalts her as the special patroness of bees

'Legend has it that she lived in Ballyvourney on the mountains between Kerry and Cork, and that the first bees in Ireland were brought to her by Saint Modmnoc of Cambria (who had been given them by St David) in a *beachaire* or square box made to hold bees. This the saint had in her hand when a band of robbers approached, threatening to destroy the chieftain's lands and dwellings in his absence. The saint went out to entreat them to forgo their pillaging, but they would not listen to her. Then Gobnat opened the box containing the bees leaving the doors ajar. One by one they escaped until "the air was brown with their bodies". The robber band were terrified, and turning their horses, fled.'

Sister Mary Donatus, *Beasts and Birds in the Lives of the Early Irish Saints*, 1934

St Brigid's, St Gobnat's and St Patrick's: the three cold feasts of the year.

In Wales and Ireland the season for netting salmon on inland waters begins

'New boats are made each year, woven of withies on a frame of hazel rods cut in the autumn after the leaves have fallen and allowed to season over winter, and the whole covered with an ox-hide. Such boats are light and easy to manoeuvre.'

J. Hornell, *British Coracles and Irish Curraghs*, 1938

The Adventures of Teigue, son of Cian

'The project which Teigue formed was to build and fit out (suitably to a long passage) a smart, strongly put together currach of five and twenty thwarts, in which should be forty ox-hides of hard bark-soaked red leather. Then he provided all due items of his currach's necessaries: in the way of thick tall masts, of broad-bladed oars, of pilots fully qualified, and of thwarts solidly well laid and fitted in their berths, in such fashion that in all respects this currach was as it should be and thoroughly staunch.'

Book of Lismore, Irish, fifteenth century

'Brendan fasted forty days and did hard penance. And he made a very large ship having strong hides nailed over it, and pitch over the hides, that the water would not come in.'

Voyage of Brendan, edited by Lady Gregory, 1907

It was believed in parts of Wales that if a baby cried at its baptism, it would grow up to be a good singer

'... the weather fearful, violent deadly E. wind and the hardest frost we have had yet ... when I got to the Chapel my beard mustaches and whiskers were so stiff with ice that I could hardly open my mouth and my beard was frozen on to my mackintosh. There was a large christening party from Llwyn Gwilym. The baby was baptised in ice which was broken and swimming about in the font.'

Revd Francis Kilvert, *Diary*, 13 February 1870

Lupercalia or the Feast of Valentine the martyr: a day for Cornish lovers and smokers

'Pengrouze, a lad in many a science blest,
Outshone his toning brothers of the west:
Of smugling, hurling, wrestling much he knew,
And much of tin, and much of pilchards too.
Fam'd at each village, town, and country-house,
Menacken, Helstone, Polkinhorne, and Grouze;
Trespissen, Buddock, Cony-yerle, Treverry,
Polbastard, Hallabazzack, Eglesderry
Pencob, and Restijeg, Treviskey, Breague,
Irewinnick, Buskenwyn, Busveal, Roscreague:
But what avail'd his fame and various art,
Since he, by love, was smitten to the heart?
The shaft a beam of Bet Polglaze's eyes;
And now he dumplin' loaths, and pilchard pies.
Young was the lass, a servant at St Tizzy,
Born at Polpiss, and bred at Mevagizzy
Calm o'er the mountain blush'd the rising day,
And ting'd the summit with a purple ray,
When sleepless from his hutch the lover stole,
And met, by chance, the mistress of his soul.
And "Whither go'st?" he scratched his skull and cry'd;
"Arrear, God bless us," well the nymph reply'd,
"To Yealston sure to buy a pound o' backy,
That us and measter wonderfully lacky;
God bless us ale, this fortnight, 'pon my word,
We nothing smoaks but oak leaves and cue-terd."'

James Halliwell, *Dictionary of Archaic and Provincial Words*, 1847

February

15

February is ash month

'Dark is the colour of the ash: timber that makes the wheels to go; rods he furnishes for horsemen's hands, and his form turns battle into flight.'

'Death of Fergus', Irish, early sixteenth century, B.L. Egerton MS 1782

Ernest Henry Shackleton was born in Ireland on 15 February 1874.

The *Endurance* expedition to the Antarctic was in respect of its aims an utter failure: the ship was abandoned and later crushed by the ice, the party was marooned for eight months on diminishing floes, no one knew where they were and there was no hope of rescue. But it was no failure in its achievements. Shackleton and five of his men crossed nearly one thousand miles of the wildest sea in the world in an open boat, missed their target of the South Georgian whaling station and had to walk across the trackless wastes of South Georgia without equipment to reach the station and help for their stranded colleagues, of whom not one died.

16

The dangers of ploughing

'The crop will be all oats when sown in February, it will be straw and oats when sown in March, it will be wisps and chaff-bags when sown in April.'

Irish saying

'Most of their land is used for pasture. They cultivate very little of it, growing a few flowers and sowing a plot here and there. They use oxen to pull their ploughs and carts, sometimes in pairs but more often four at a time. The ploughman walks in front, but backwards. When the bull pulls out of the yoke, as often happens, he falls on his back and is in grave danger.'

Gerald of Wales, *Description of Wales*, late twelfth century

In praise of Fermanagh

'The paradise of Ireland is Fermanagh, the peaceful fruitful plain, the land of bright dry smooth fields, in form like the shores of Heaven.'

Tadgh Dall Ó hUiginn (1550–1591), translated by Kenneth Hurlstone Jackson

James 'Ossian' MacPherson, born in Invernesshire, died this day in 1796, and is buried in Poets' Corner, Westminster Abbey

MacPherson was the alleged translator of the Ossianic poems, 'Fingal' and others, which were published in the 1760s. Republished as *Poems of Ossian* in 1807, they were denounced as unhistorical plagiarisms. But he certainly collected oral literature in the Highlands and Isles, and, though he referred to manuscripts, 'he never seriously exerted himself to rebut the charge of forgery'.

Dictionary of National Biography, 1893

'The Daughter of Dunthalmo wept in silence, the fair-haired, blue-eyed Colmal.* Her eye had rolled in secret on Calthon; his loveliness swelled in her soul. She trembled for her warrior; but what could Colmal do? Her arm could not lift the spear; nor was the sword formed for her side. Her white breast never rose beneath a mail. Neither was her eye the terror of heroes. What canst thou do, O Colmal for the falling chief?'

[*Colmal: a woman with small eyebrows]

'Calthon and Colmal, a Poem by Ossian (son of Fionn MacUmhal)', 1762

Saint Colman, Bishop of Lindisfarne died AD 676

Saint Colman returned to Ireland with his monks after the Synod of Whitby in AD 663 or 664, when he lost the dispute over the Celtic and Roman use of keeping Easter. They went to Inishbofin off the coast of Connaught, but he found that his English monks complained that the Irishmen expected them to do all the work, so took them to another monastery in Mayo.

'There are so many Colmans in the Irish martyrologies that it is sometimes hard to distinguish them. In the Life of St Carthage it is said that once, when some of his monks were working near a stream their foreman cried "Colman, get into the water", and twelve jumped in.'

Alban Butler, *Lives of the Saints*, 1756–9

'Another Colman, son of Duach, was anciently commemorated on February 3rd: it was he who had three pets, a cock, a mouse and a midge, all of whom rendered him unique services. The cock woke him in time for offices, the mouse nibbled his ears until he got up, and the midge kept his place in the book he was reading.'

Revd Sabine Baring-Gould, *Lives of the Saints*, 1877

February

Season of grey blasts

'From the east comes the crimson wind, from the south the white, from the north the black and from the west the grey.'

'Seanchas Mór', Irish, *c.* eighth century

'South winds, heat and plenty cling
West winds fish and milk will bring
North winds bringeth gales and snow
East winds mean more fruit will grow.'

T. D. MacDonald, *Gaelic Proverbs and Proverbial Sayings*, 1926

Grow the savoy cabbage variety 'Celtic'

'Let us kill the pig and make a good dressing of cabbage to go with it as a proper diet for the grey touch of early Spring.'

Celtic Review, 1905–6

'A February calm or a Dog Days' wind
Never will be lasting.'

Irish saying

Pisces

In Pisces they who shall be born shall have enmity: he who takes to his bed is healed and his feet and soles suffer most; he who takes to flight finds not cause.

Apostle: Thaddeus
Ruler: Cocus
Medieval Irish Zodiac, Basle Library

Cure for sore feet

For soreness under the toes from walking barefoot, apply as dressing little shreds of wool found on the hill and still full of natural grease. For a sore place, as a cut where a shoe rubs, apply ribwort (*Slánlus* – herb of health – is its name in Gaelic).

Old Cures of South Uist

Calculating the date of Easter

'Easter forced itself on men's notice as a visible sign of discord, since the sudden transition from the gloom of Holy Week to the rejoicings of the Day of Resurrection was an event in the Christian year to catch the attention of the most careless, and to see one Christian still keeping the Lenten fast while another at his side was in the midst of the Easter revels brought out in the clearest fashion how far they were from dwelling as brethren in unison together. In this way it came about that as the result of one rule, the Celtic Easter often anticipated the Roman by a week, while occasionally, through the operation of another, it would fall no less than four weeks later. Among the Celts 25th March was the earliest possible Easter Day, 21st April the latest, while at Rome the range of oscillation was from 22nd March to 25th April. As a result of these conflicting calculations, it was the exception for the two Easters to coincide.'

Sir John Edward Lloyd, *A History of Wales*, 1911

Quadragesima falls about now: it is the last chance to marry before Lent

On Shrove Tuesday it is customary to have *sollaghyn* or crowdy for dinner, instead of breakfast as at other times; and for supper, meat, with a large pudding and pancakes. Into the latter are thrown a ring and a piece of silver money, with which the candidates for matrimony try their fortune.

The Sunday before Lent and Shrove Tuesday were called Runaway Sunday and Galloping Tuesday respectively.

Shrovetide is the name given to the days immediately preceding Ash Wednesday which were anciently days of preparation for the penitential time of Lent, as indeed the whole period after Septuagesima Sunday appears to have been. After confession, the faithful, on the eve of entering Lent, were indulged with permission to give themselves up to amusements.

February

Shrovetide

Shrove: in Welsh, *Ynyd*; in Old Irish, *Init*; in Manx, *Ynnyd*; from the Latin *initium*.

'It is still customary on certain estates to make annual payments to the landlord called *Ynyd*, or *Gieir Ynyd*, usually consisting of one hen and twenty eggs. In one case brought before the Commission the payment was of two fat geese and forty eggs.'

Minutes of Evidence, Welsh Land Commission, 1895

Competitions were held at Shrovetide where (hard-boiled) eggs were struck against each other, end to end, until only one egg remained unbroken: this was called 'egg-shackling' in Cornwall, and 'dumping eggs' in Cumbria. Near Dublin the eggs were shaken together in a sieve.

To make pancakes: eggs, flour and sugar must be baked into the 'sautie' bannock in silence to make 'dumb cake'.

Nickanan Night

Tonight is called 'Nickanan Night' in Cornwall. Wild antics take place – people throwing water, rubbing soot, carrying away doors and gates – before Lenten sobriety properly begins.

'Fair weather at Shrovetide is foul weather at Easter and vice versa.'

Highland saying

'At Tréguier the magpie begins her nest on the 24 February, and lays an egg on Good Friday.'

Breton proverb

'Nest at Brigid, egg at Shrove, chick at Easter.'

Alexander Carmichael, *Carmina Gadelica*, 1900

Lent will begin about now: too late for marriage until after Easter

'There was great sport in them days, boys and girls going round sporting and singing and dancing. We were all like the one family. My wife was a nice dancer. I kept from all the girls as well as I could because I was afraid of them. I seen 21 marriages above at the old chapel on a Shrove Tuesday. The Bishop here put a tax on the runaway couples. They'd have to come to the chapel, and the priest would call them out and ask them if they were sorry, and they'd say they were. The man would say he was; and she'd be at home. They were love matches. He used to bring her to some friend's house and send word to her people.'
Michael Gaynor of Elphin, County Roscommon, tailor, born 1845,
Article in *Béaloideas*, 1937

'On Ash Wednesday the old woman changes her conduct.'
Breton proverb

The stonechat is a fine musician, and a watchful bird

He is the bird with the sharpest eye and keenest ear in the bird world. He has got lore of the weather from the man in the moon, knowledge of the earth from the old woman of night (the owl), and skill of the ocean from the maiden of the sea. He comes and none knows whence; he goes and none knows whither; he will be to you a guide to your heart's desire.
Scottish lore

Harry Lauder, the Scottish hero of the music hall who composed and sang such songs as 'Stop Yer Ticklin' Jock' and 'I Loved a Lassie', was born in 1870 and died this day in 1950.

Lauder is a small town in Berwickshire, where, in 1482, the fifth Earl of Angus hanged the Earl of Mar and other favourites of King James III, earning himself the nickname 'Archibald Bell-the-Cat'.

February

Look for the first appearance of nature's tobacco and matches

Coltsfoot (*galla'n greanchair,* Irish; *Troed yr Ebol, Pesychlys*, Welsh; *Tussilago farfara*, Latin) grows abundantly, especially on low-lying, clay soils, and flowers from February to April, though its leaves begin to appear in March.

The dried leaves, collected in June and smoked like tobacco, are a cure for coughs, wheezes and shortness of breath; the crushed leaves are rubbed on the skin for insect bites and burns; before matches were invented the down on the back of the leaves was harvested to be made into tinder.

Bretons spent long winter evenings reducing tobacco to a fine powder, which they kept in a *chinchoire* made of ox horn, with a screw cap at the point.

An eclipse

In 1652 '. . . there was a great ecclipse of the sun about 9 hours in the forenoon on a monday; the earth was much darkened, the lyke, as thought by astrologers, was not since the darkness at our Lord's Passion. The country-people teeling loused their plews, and thought it had been the latter day: Some of the starrs were seen, it fell so dark, and birds clapt to the ground.'

Revd Mr Robert Law, *Memorialls; or the Memorable Things that fell out within this Island of Brittain from 1638–1684*

[Editor's note, 1819: 'The day of this eclipse is still denominated by the common people of Scotland "the Mirk Monday."']

'The wild Irish, or Welch, who during Eclipses run about beating etc. Pans thinking their clamour and vexations availeable to the assistance of the higher Orbes.'

John Aubrey, *Remaines of Gentilisme and Judaisme*, 1688

The Old Style Calendar was introduced by Julius Caesar in AD 45

Known as the Julian Calendar, it set up a year of 365 days, with an extra day every fourth year, on the sixth calends of March, or 24 February. In 1582, Pope Gregory XIII ordered the use of a reformed, or New Style calendar.

The word *biseach*, as in *Lá Bhisigh* (the intercalary day), and *Bliadhain bhisigh* (leap year), means increase, improvement or profit, hence the adage *chomh biseamhail le cataibh*, 'as prolific as cats'.

One of these was the vicious kitten that grew into *Cath Palug*, Palug's cat: the wild cat of Anglesey, which feasted on his rescuer's sons.

'The Irish have always looked on cats as evil and mysteriously connected with some demoniacal influence. On entering a house the usual salutation is, "God save all here, except the cat." Even the cake on the griddle may be blessed, but no one says, "God bless the cat." '

Lady Wilde, *Ancient Legends of Ireland*, 1888

MARCH

the busy month

Breton: *Meurs*   Cornish: *Merth*
Irish: *Márta*   Manx: *Mayrnt*
Scottish: *A Mhárt*   Welsh: *Mawrth*

The festival of St David, patron saint of Wales, known as 'the waterman' for his asceticism

'St David who was of royal extraction, and uncle to King Arthur, died, aged a hundred and forty-six years, on the first of March, still celebrated by the Welsh, perchance to perpetuate the memory of his abstinence, whose contented mind made many a favourite meal on such roots of the earth.'

The Episcopal Almanack for 1677

'I like the leeke above all herbes and flowers.
When first we wore the same the field was ours.
The Leeke is white and greene, wherby is ment
That Britanes are both stout and eminent;
Next to the Lion and the Unicorn,
The Leeke the fairest emblyn that is worne.'

'A Collection of Pedigrees', B.L. Harleian MS

The virtues of the leek

'The juice is good against the vomiting of blood. It is good for women who desire children to eat leeks. Take leeks and wine to cure the bite of adders and venomous beasts. The juice of leeks and woman's milk is good against pneumonia. The juice with goat's gall and honey in equal parts, put warm into the ear, is good for deafness. It will relieve wind of the stomach, and engender strange dreams.'

Meddygon Myddfai, Welsh, thirteenth century

A Flintshire recipe

Scald some leeks for a few minutes in boiling water and then stew them slowly in milk until tender. With this milk, a little butter and some flour make a sauce, adding cream and an egg-yolk just before pouring over the leeks.

March

At St David's the first three days of March were sacred to the honour of Saints David, Nun (or Non, David's mother) and Lily

'If any of the people had been known to work upon any of these Days, it would have been esteemed a very heinous Offence.'

Brown Willis, *Survey of St David's*, 1717

St Nun's Well

St Nun's Well afforded 'a very singular manner of curing madness, in the parish of Altarnun – to place the disordered in mind on the brink of a square pool, filled with water from St Nun's Well. The patient, having no intimation of what was intended, was, by a sudden blow on the breast, tumbled into the pool, where he was tossed up and down by some persons of superior strength, till, being quite debilitated, his Fury forsook him; he was then carried to Church, and certain Masses sung over him. The Cornish call this Immersion *Boossening*, from *Beuzi* or *Bidhyzi* signifying to dip or drown.'

William Borlase, *Natural History of Cornwall*, 1758

William Price of Llantrisant, a noted eccentric, was born on 4 March 1800 in the parish of Rudry, Monmouthshire

An advocate of free love and vegetarianism and an opponent of vivisection and the Church, Price claimed to be the Archdruid, and wore a fox-skin head-dress whilst performing ancient rites on the Pontypridd rocking stone.

'Much has been written about Druids' dress, their ornaments, and the mysteries of their craft, – as the glass boat, the cup, the cross, etc. Archdruid Myfyr, at Pontypridd (not Dr Price), explained to the present writer, his processional cross, with movable arms; his wonderful egg, bequeathed from past ages; his *Penthynen*, writing rods, or staff book; his rosary, – used by ancient priests, not less than by modern Mahometans and Christians; his glass beads; his *torque* for the neck; his breastplate of judgment; his crescent adornments; his staff of office, etc.'

James Bonwick, *Irish Druids and Old Irish Religions*, 1894

The seed of the eringo (the sea holly) will procure sleep, but do not take too much

This plant is also said to relieve impotence.

'This, the first Friday in March, is another tinners' holiday. It is marked by a serio-comic custom of sending a boy to the highest hillock of the works and allowing him to sleep there as long as he can, the length of his sleep to be the measure of the afternoon nap of the tinners throughout the ensuing twelve months. Lide is an obsolete term for the month of March and is preserved in old proverbs, such as, for example, "Ducks won't lay till they've drunk Lide water."'

Miss M. A. Courtney, *Cornish Feasts and Feasten Customs*, 1886

Ember Days in the first week of Lent – there should be no merrymaking

In Ireland the austerity of Lent was strictly observed; no meat, eggs, butter, or milk. As most bread was made with buttermilk people had to be content with oatcakes made with oatmeal (better if a little flour is sifted into it), a big pinch of salt, baking powder and water, all mixed and 'hardened' on a griddle over a fire, (or, in a gas oven, at mark 4 for twenty-five minutes). When the restrictions of Lent have been removed, add butter or lard to the water, boil and then mix into the dry ingredients; delicious with honey.

'Bright and clear early and all day and warm at 1. Walked over to 244's position with Colonel and then up to 234 beyond Dainville station, and listened to larks and watched aeroplane fights. 2 planes down, one in flames, a Hun. Some 10 of our planes together very high. Shells into Arras in afternoon.'

Edward Thomas (1878–1917), Diary, 6 March 1917

March

7 Never abuse the provider of food

The skin of the 'master-otter' gives protection against fire, shipwreck, and will prevent steel and bullet from harming the man who carries even a small scrap of the precious material. But he himself has preservative qualities, as he cannot be harmed by mortal hands.

The otter is called *Dobor chú*, 'water-dog', in Irish; *dyfrgi*, in Welsh.

'Saint Coemgen was in Cell Iffin during Lent, where every day an otter brought a salmon to feed himself and his company, until one day it occurred to the monk Cellch that he could make a fine glove of his skin. The otter, though a mere brute beast, understood his thought and from that time ceased to perform this useful service.'

Sister Mary Donatus, *Beasts and Birds in the Lives of the Early Irish Saints*, 1934

'On March the seventh the day lengthens with an ox-stride.'

Breton proverb

8 Hibernating animals are not quite awake yet

'When you live a life of intense activity for six months in the year, and of comparative or actual somnolence for the other six, during the latter period you cannot be continually pleading sleepiness when there are people about or things to be done. The excuse gets monotonous.'

Kenneth Grahame, *The Wind in the Willows*, 1908

Kenneth Grahame, admirer of badgers, later gentleman clerk in the Bank of England and author, was born in Edinburgh this day in 1859.

Nettle tops, eaten in spring, will banish the phlegmatic superfluities left in the body of man by the cold wet winter. A spring tonic may also be made with the seeds of the same plant, mixed with pepper, wine and honey.

The bittern, that rare and elusive bird, may return to its nest in the reed beds at the end of winter

Called 'bumpy corse' (*Bwmpygors*, 'boom of the marsh') or 'boom bird' in Wales, 'bog drum' in Ireland and Scotland and 'clabitter' in Cornwall, the bittern is now rarely heard, and more rarely seen.

'It's not for the common birds that I'd mourn,
The black-bird, the corn-crake or the crane
But for the bittern that's shy and apart
And drinks in the marsh from the lone bog-
     drain.

In a wintering island by Constantine's halls
A bittern calls from a wineless place,
And tells me that hither he cannot come
Till the summer is here and the sunny days.'

Cathal Buidhe Mac Giolla Ghunna, *c.* 1750, translated by
Thomas MacDonagh

The meaning of March

Màrt in Scottish Gaelic means: month of March; Tuesday; time suitable for agricultural work; busiest time at anything; great haste; and seed time.

'The old "months" appear to have been movable, and depended for the time of their commencement on whether the suitable weather had arrived. If the weather hadn't come, neither had the month, e.g *Luath no mall g'an tig am Naigh, thig a' chubhag,* – "Late or early as May comes so comes the cuckoo."'

Edward Dwelly, *The Illustrated Gaelic Dictionary*, 1911

'One cannot say here, as elsewhere, that the farmer's toil is one long round. They plough the soil once in March and April for oats, a second time in summer, and then they turn it a third time while the grain is being threshed.'

Gerald of Wales, *Description of Wales*, late twelfth century

March

11 Making a field

'The other day the man of this house made a new field. The old man and his eldest son dug out the clay, with the care of men working a gold-mine, and Michael packed it in panniers for transport to a flat rock in a sheltered corner of the holding, where it was mixed with sand and seaweed and spread out in a layer upon the shore.'

J. M. Synge, *The Aran Islands*, 1907

'I think premiums for the best plots of early potatoes, white turnips, cabbages, &c., &c., should be offered by the Board, and if this course was adopted the industry would probably get a fair start.'

Major Robert Ruttledge-Fair, Inspector, *Report on the Aran Islands to the Congested Districts Board for Ireland*, 1893

12 St David's Day, Old Style: good and bad qualities in the Welsh

'The Walsh men be hardy men, stronge men, & goodly men; they woulde be exalted, & they do set muche by theyr kyndred and prophecyes; and many of them be lovynge and kyndharted, faythful, & vertuous. And there be many of them the whyche be lyght fyngered, & loveth a purse; but this matter latly is reformed. but lechery in manye places is to much used, Wherfore ther be many bastards openly knowen; and many prestes sonnes aboundeth in the countre, specially in North Wales; but that is nowe refomed, considring the restriction of the kynges actes, that prestes shal have no concubynes.'

Andrew Boorde, *The Fyrst Boke of the Introduction of Knowledge*

'The Welsh go to extremes in all matters. You may never find anyone worse than a bad Welshman, but you will certainly never find anyone better than a good one.'

Gerald of Wales, *Description of Wales*, late twelfth century

Barnacle geese might be eaten during Lent, as it was believed that they were the progeny of shellfish

'They are like marsh geese, but smaller. At first they appear as excrescences on fir-logs carried down upon the waters. Then they hang by their beaks from what seems like seaweed clinging to the log, while their bodies, to allow for their more unimpeded development, are enclosed in shells.'

Gerald of Wales, *The History and Topography of Ireland, c.* 1187

'Because they are not hatched in the manner of birds people eat them salted during Lent.'

Bartholomaeus Chassanaeus, *Catalogus Gloriae Mundi*, 1617

'I am informed that in Brittany barnacles are still allowed to be eaten on Fridays, and that the Roman Catholic Bishop of Ferns may give permission to people out of his diocese to eat these birds at table.'

Max Nuller, *The Science of Language*, 1891

The beginning of the breeding season

'Birds go mating in the spring of the year, and ewes at the leaves falling, but a young girl must have her lover in all the course of the sun and moon.'

J. M. Synge, *Deirdre of the Sorrows*, 1910

'Infant's flesh will be in season throughout the year, but more plentiful in March, and a little before and after, for we are told by a grave Author, and eminent French physician [Rabelais], that Fish being a prolifick Dyet, there are more children born in Roman Catholick Countries about Nine Months after Lent, than at any other season.'

Jonathan Swift, *A Modest Proposal*, 1729 in which Swift suggests that the poor might be relieved by selling their numerous children as food for the rich.

March

15

Look out for the useful blue-purple ground ivy, now beginning to flower

Ground ivy or ale-hoof (*Glechoma hederacea*), a common and pleasantly pungent ground-creeper, was used to cure deafness, bronchitis and eye complaints.

'Take juice of ground ivy and woman's milk, equal parts of each. Strain through fine linen, and put a drop in the painful eye.'

'For an opacity of the eye. Let some ground ivy juice be put therein, and the opacity will be removed, the eye becoming spotless and clear.'

Meddygon Myddfai, Welsh, thirteenth century

Also used, before the days of hops, to clear, preserve and flavour ale, hence its names 'alehoof' and the Welsh *llysiau'r gerwyn*, 'herbs of the (ale) vat'.

'The women of our Northern parts, especially about Wales and Cheshire, do tun the herbe Ale hoove into their ale ... being tunned up in ale and drunk, it also purgeth the head from rheumatic humour flowing from the brain.'

Gerard, *Herball*, 1597

16

Dreams of food in the Lenten fast

' "And what is thy own name, if we
    may ask?"
"Not hard to tell," said the phantom.
"Wheatlet, son of Milklet,
Son of juicy Bacon,
Is mine own name.
Honey Butter-roll
Is the man's name
Who bears my bag.

Haunch of Mutton
Is my dog's name,
Of lovely leaps.
Lard, my wife,
Sweetly smiles
Across the kale-top.

Cheese-curds, my daughter,
Goes round the spit,
Fair is her fame.
Corned Beef, my son,
Whose mantle shines
Over a big tail.

Beef-lard, my steed,
An excellent stallion,
That increases studs;
A guard against toil
Is the saddle on cheese
On his back." '

The Vision of Mac Conglinne, Irish, fourteenth century, edited by Kuno Meyer, 1892

St Patrick's Day

'Repose of Patrick on the 16th of the Kalends of April [17 March] in the 432nd year from the Passion of the Lord.'
Annals of Innisfallen for AD 496

'As the sturgeon swims in midstream so St Patrick's Day falls exactly in mid-Spring.'
Irish saying

'Then Patrick chanted mass and blessed the rath of Drumderg in which Fionn Mac Cumall had been. The clerics saw Caeilte and his band draw near, and fear fell on them before the tall men with their huge wolfhounds, for they were not people of one epoch with the clergy.

Then Calpurn's son Patrick, apostle of the Gael, rose and took the aspergillum to sprinkle holy water on the great men over whom there had been floating until that day a thousand legions of demons.'
'The Colloquy of the Old Men', Irish, thirteenth century, translated by Kuno Meyer

Patrick Brontë was born 17 March 1777 in Ballynaskeagh, Co. Down, son of Hugh Brunty. He died in Haworth, Yorkshire, having survived all his children, on 7 June 1861.

Snake Stones

'I have sene stones the whiche have had the forme and shap of a snake and other venimous wormes. And the people of the countre sayth that suche stones were wormes, and they were turned into stones by the power of God and the prayers of saynt Patryk. And Englysh marchauntes of England do fetch of the erth of Irlonde to caste in their gardens, to kepe out and to kyll venimous wormes.'
Andrew Boorde, *The Fyrste Boke of the Introduction of Knowledge*

March

Tobias Smollett was born at Dalquhern, Dumbartonshire, in 1721

'The humorous, arrogant, red-headed, stiff-necked, thin-skinned, scurrilous, brilliant, Scots hack of genius' was also a physician, sometime ship's doctor and a pioneer novelist.

'I find by your tongues you are from Scotland, gentlemen. My grandmother by the father's side was of your country; and I am so prepossessed in its favour that I never meet a Scotchman but my heart warms. The Scots are very brave people. There is scarce a great family in the kingdom that cannot boast of some exploits performed by its ancestors many hundred years ago. There's your Douglases, Gordons, Campbells, Hamiltons. We have no such ancient families here in England. Then you are all very well educated. I have known a pedlar talk in Greek and Hebrew, as well as they had been his mother tongue.'

Tobias Smollett, *Roderick Random*, 1748

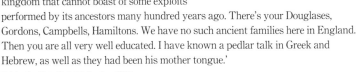

Industrious little people

'The first of March let pass
The second of March if need be;
But the third of March
Though you could not send a stone
A nail's breadth against the north wind
Sow your seed in March.'

T. D. Macdonald, *Gaelic Proverbs and Proverbial Sayings*, 1926

In the Old Style calendar, the third week of March corresponds to the New Style first week of April.

'In the Old Welsh legends there is a story of a man who was told to recover every grain of seed that had been sown in a large field, and bring it all in without one missing by sunset. He came to an ant-hill and enlisted the sympathies of the industrious little people. They spread all over the field and before sundown the seed was all in except one grain, and as the sun was setting over the western skies a lame ant hobbled along with that grain also.'

David Lloyd George (1863–1945), Welsh Nationalist and British Prime Minister, 1916–18, in a recruiting speech of 1915

Spring Equinox: the sun moves from south to north across the celestial equator

'The day increases in pleasant manner and the night lessens from the festival of fair-flanked Thomas in the East to the festival of dumb Faolan.
The night increases, it is no lie, and every day diminishes; from the festival of Faolan, look forward to the festival of Thomas once more.
At the festival of mighty Benedict on the 12th Kalends April, that is the festival you compute, it is no lie, which is of equal length both day and night.'

'The Calendar of Oengus', Irish, ninth century

'Schyting* and shynning is good March weather.'

[*skyte – a sudden shower]

Fergusson, *Scottish Proverbs*, 1641

Aries

In Aries he who goes to bed shall be long distressed, and his head mostly suffers. they that shall be born are likely to live; he who takes to flight will return of his own accord. The Moons leap.

Apostle: John

Ruler: Occianus

Medieval Irish Zodiac, Basle Library

'John McLoranan said he knew the late Lord Masserecne when he was a boy, and remembers that he met with a fall from his horse which injured him so much that he ever afterwards appeared to be weak in his judgment.
He used to walk very oddly, with his arms across and his hands upon his shoulders. He said he did this because he wished to grow stout, and if he confined himself in one way it would break out in another.'

Belfast Telegraph, March 1809

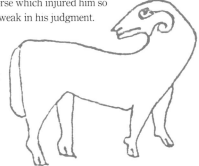

The greatest philosopher the Western World produced between Augustine and Aquinas was a ninth-century Irishman

The Papal librarian to Charles the Bald, describing a work of translation by Eriugena: 'It is a wonderful thing how that barbarian, living at the ends of the earth, who might be supposed to be as far removed from the knowledge of this other language as he is from the familiar use of it, has been able to comprehend such ideas and translate them into another tongue: I refer to John Scotigena, whom I have learned by report to be in all things a holy man.'

MS Florence Biblioteca Laurentiana Plut. 89

'Johannes Erigena, surnamed Scotus, a man renowned for Learning, sitting at the Table in respect of his Learning with Charles the Bauld, Emperour and King of France, behaved himself as a slovenly Scholar, nothing courtly; whereupon the Emperour asked him merrily, "Quid interest inter Scotum et Sotum" – "What is the difference between a Scot and a Sot?" He merrily, but yet malapertly answered, "Mensa", "The Table", as though the Emperour were the Sot and he the Scot.'

William Camden, *Remains Concerning Britain*, 1684

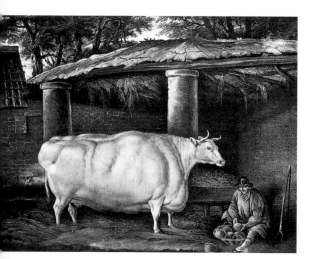

Gorse time

'Kissing's out of season when gorse is out of bloom.'

Irish saying

Gorse, furze or whin, comes into full flower in March, but the shrub is almost never out of flower.

The custom of growing a field of whins to provide winter fodder for horses and cattle is almost forgotten. It was done in the eastern highlands of Scotland, the midlands of Ireland and the poorer parts of Brittany until at least the 1950s. The whins were bruised and pounded, or 'melled', with a wooden maul (*cnotag*) on flat slabs of stone, or stone basins.

Lady Day: the sea grows warmer today and the healing herbs start to grow

'From the 8th Kalends of glorious April to the 3rd Kalends of July, at that time, it is no great contention, it is the top of every herb that heals.

From the 8th Kalends of July after that to the 8th Kalends October, the stalk of every herb, a deed without prohibition, it is that which heals every distress.

The root of every herb, it is true, from the 8th Kalends October, Diancecht ordained it in his wisdom, to the 8th Kalends of noble April.

Thee hundred and sixty-five herbs, that is their number, it is no great untruth, the herbs of every sickness, verses tell of it; let them all be plucked on the 8th Kalends.'

Irish, early sixteenth century, B.L. Add. 30512

'Never tell your dreams until you have broken your fast, and always tell them first to a woman called Mary.'

Irish saying

As mad as a March hare?

'Hares are considered unlucky, as the witches constantly assume their form in order to gain entrance to a field where they can bewitch the cattle.'

Lady Wilde, *Ancient Legends of Ireland*, 1888

In Ireland: 'The bodies of all animals, wild beasts, and birds, are smaller in their species than anywhere else. Only men retain their full size. There is a remarkable thing about their hares: if they are put up by dogs, they always try, unlike other hares, to make their escape in cover, as does the fox, – in hidden country, and not in the open. They never make for the plains or rocky paths unless they are compelled to it.'

Gerald of Wales, *The History and Topography of Ireland, c.* 1187

Beware travel at this time, lest you encounter house-moving fairies

'They remove to other Lodgings at the Beginning of each Quarter of the Year, so traversing till Doomsday, being impotent of staying in one Place, and finding some Ease by so Journeying and changing Habitations. Their chameleon-like Bodies swim in the Air near the Earth with Bag and Baggage, and at such Times Men of Second Sight have very terrifying Encounters with them, even on High Ways. Who therefore shun to travel abroad at these Seasons, and thereby have made it a Custom among the Scottish–Irish to keep Church duly every first Sunday of the Quarter to fene or hallow themselves, their Corns and Cattle from these wandering Tribes. And many of these superstitious People will not be seen in Church again until the next Quarter begin.'

Robert Kirk, Minister at Aberfoyle, *The Secret Commonwealth*, 1691

'When going into a new house everyone should bring a gift, however small, and should take nothing away.'

Irish saying

Peel Fair day in the Isle of Man

Summer visitors

'He watched their flight; bird after bird: a bright dark flash, a swerve, a flutter of wings. He tried to count them before all their darting quivering bodies passed: six, ten, eleven: and wondered were they odd or even in number. Twelve, thirteen: for two came wheeling down from the upper sky. They were flying high and low, but ever round and round in straight and curving lines and ever flying from left to right, circling about a temple of air.'

James Joyce, *A Portrait of the Artist as a Young Man*, 1916

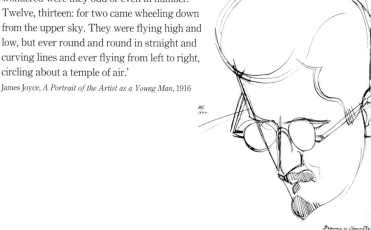

Drawing of James Joyce by Wyndham Lewis

The days of the brindled cow: *Laetheanta na riaibhche*

'I heard when I was young that an old cow rejoiced when March was out, threw up her heels and said: "March is gone now and I'll be alright!"

March heard what the old cow said and borrowed three days from April and killed the old cow. These three days are still called in my district "The Borrowin' Days".'

Article by Patrick Duffy of County Longford in *Béaloideas*, 1932

Keep snakeskins carefully

'When the moon is in her first increase, under the sign called Aries, or the Ram, which falls in the month of March, on the third day of the calends of April, when the first seed under this sign are formed, then burn the skin of a snake, which has been cast in the time of harvest. Take the ashes and keep them carefully, for they are the most precious application which any human tongue can order. Let the first instance at hand suffice: whosoever has a fresh wound, let him cover it with a little of this ash, and it will heal in three days.'

Meddygon Myddfai, Welsh, thirteenth century

March

31

St Kessock's Day

'On St Kessock's Day every eel is pregnant.'

T. D. Macdonald, *Gaelic Proverbs and Proverbial Sayings*, 1926

The Island Magee witches

'The last trial for witchcraft was held in Ireland at Carrickfergus on this date in 1711. The persons accused were alleged to have tormented a young girl at a house in Island Magee, long believed to have been haunted, where she had found an apron, missing for a long time, on the parlour floor, and had loosened the five strange knots with which it was tied. The next day she was gripped by a pain in her thigh and fell into a fit, and on recovery found herself tormented by several women while strange noises and stranger happenings filled the house. The accused women, able to repeat the Lord's Prayer, had the sympathy of the judge but not of the jury who found them guilty: the prisoners were sentenced to twelve months' imprisonment and four exposures to the displeasure of the populace in the pillory of Carrickfergus.'

Samuel MacSkimin, *History of Carrickfergus*, 1811

APRIL
the primrose month

Breton: *Imbrel, Ebrel* Cornish: *Ebral*
Irish: *Aibrean* Manx: *Averil*
Scottish: *Giblean* Welsh: *Ebrill*

April

1

In April the swallow, the cuckoo and the corncrake arrive, but winter lingers, an uninvited guest

'The month of April, the upland is misty,
the oxen are weary, the earth is bare,
feeble is the stag, playful the long-eared;*
usual is a guest though he be not invited;
everyone has many faults where he is not loved;
blessed is he that is faithful;
usual is destruction upon the children of the wicked;
usual after arrogance is lasting death.'

[*hare]

Welsh, late fifteenth century, translated by K. H. Jackson

2

On this day in 1902, Maud Gonne was Caithleen ní Houlihan in W. B. Yeats's play

She had the 'walk of a queen', and created a sensation. Loved by Yeats, she turned down his proposal of marriage (as, later, did her daughter, Iseult).

'Oh Maud, why don't you marry me and give up this tragic struggle and live a peaceful life? I could make such a beautiful life for you among artists and writers who would understand you.'
'Poets should never marry. The world should thank me for not marrying you.'
Maud Gonne MacBride, *A Servant of the Queen*, 1938

Instead, in February 1903, she married John MacBride (who was executed in Kilmainham Jail on 5 May 1916 for his part in the Easter Rising), and produced a son, Sean, a founder of Amnesty International whose work was recognized in 1974 by the award of a Nobel peace prize.

Lenten commons

'She was a strict observer, for self and servants, of Lent, and all fast-days, but not holidays. One of the maids having fainted three times the last day of Lent, to keep soul and body together, we put a morsel of roast beef into her mouth, which came from Sir Murtagh's dinner, who never fasted, not he; but somehow or other it unfortunately reached my lady's ears . . .'

Maria Edgeworth, *Castle Rackrent*, 1800

It is said in Wales that balm, which grows easily in the garden, is very good for reviving a patient from a swoon. It will also expel melancholy vapours. Mix the decoction with honey, however: the plant's lemony smell is nicer than its taste.

Needfire

Needfire, in Gaelic '*Teine-èigin*', that is, extinguishing all the fires in the neighbourhood and raising a fresh fire by the friction of two sticks from which all others were relit, was said to stay the course of a plague or murrain in cattle.

'Strathbogie was notorious for its practice of this "heathenish" custom, and the Synod of Moray in April 1649, adopted a general rule to be applied to all offenders there – raisers of needfire in the Presbytery of Strathbogie were ordained to satisfy three days in sackcloth.'

Records of the Synod of Moray, edited by William Cramond, 1906

Palm Sunday will fall about now: men and boys should wear a sprig of yew in their hats

'Palm Sunday is called in Welsh *Sul y Blodau*, "Flower Sunday". In South Wales and Monmouthshire the graves of departed forefathers and friends are tidied and decorated with flowers.'

Revd John Fisher, *The Welsh Calendar*, 1895

'[On] Palm Sunday when he was among his apostles
He caused some of them to go to the town and untie
The she-ass and to bring [her] with them, and to say readily
If folk should come to keep [her], that God had to do with her.

And Jesus commanded them, they did straightway
All his wish as he willed; the she-ass was fetched.
On her, for a seat when raiment was put
he would ride to the city to be worshipped.'

Pascon agan Arluth, 'The Passion of Our Lord', Cornish, *c.* fifteenth century, B.L. Harleian N 1782

A letter from Sir Anthony Sentleger to Henry VIII from Maynooth on this day in 1543

'. . . And assuredly I thinke that for ther feate of warre [i.e. style of fighting], which is for light scoorers [scourers], ther ar no properer horsemen in christen ground, nor more hardie nor yet that can better indure hardeness. And as to ther footemen, they have one sorte which be harnessed in mayle and bassinetts; haueing euery of them his weapon, called a sparre, moche like the axe of Towre, and they be named Galloglasse; and for the more part ther boyes beare for them thre dartes a piece, which darts they throwe or they come to the hand stripe . . . '

Menhir cults

1909: 'At Carnac, in a natural fissure in the body of the finest menhir at the head of the Alignment of Kermario, I found quite by chance, while making a very careful examination of the geological structure of the menhir, a Roman Catholic coin (or medal) of St Peter. The menhir is very tall and smoothly rounded, and there is no possible way for the coin to have fallen into the fissure by accident. I consider this evidence of a cult rendered to stones here in Brittany. And the offering of a coin to the spirit residing in a menhir is parallel to throwing coins, pins or other objects into sacred fountains, which, as we know, is an undisputed practice.'

W. Y. Evans, *The Fairy-Faith in Celtic Countries*, 1911

'It will not do to judge the power of a saint by the size of his church.'

Breton proverb

April is willow month

'The noble willow burn not, a tree sacred to poems; within his bloom bees are a-sucking, all love the little cage.'

'Death of Fergus', Irish, early sixteenth century, B.L. Egerton MS 1782

The osier or sally used for wattling or wickerwork has been used for long generations in house and boat building, weir-construction, for artists' charcoal – crosses should be made on the shoulders with a piece of burnt willow on Saint Patrick's Day, on baskets and furniture, and even coffins. The tree has darker legends attached to it: the dwarf willow was said to have been stunted in revenge for having been used to make the Cross; the willow is also the witches' tree.

April

Tenebrae Wednesday in Holy Week was called 'Spy Wednesday' in reference to the Betrayal

'There were three treacherous encounters in the Island of Britain. The first was the meeting of Mandubratius son of Lludd who gave a place of landing to the Romans; the second was the treachery of Vortigern in the plot of the Long Knives at Stonehenge. Thirdly, the meeting of Medrawd and Iddawg Corn Prydain who conspired against Arthur.'

The Triads of Britain, early medieval

' "Sir," said Sir Bors, "I dread me ever of Sir Agravaine, that waiteth you daily to do you shame and us all; and never gave my heart against no going, that ever ye went to the queen, so much as now; for I mistrust that the king is out this night from the queen because of peradventure he hath lain some watch for you and the queen, and therefore I dread me sore of treason." '

Sir Thomas Mallory, *Morte d'Arthur*, 1470

Maundy Thursday falls about now

Shear Thursday (Irish, *Caplaid*; Welsh, *Cablyd*; Latin, *Capillatio*). Celtic peoples marked this penitential time by tonsuring their heads in preparation for anointment on Easter Day.

'In old faders dayes the people wolde that day shere thyr hedes, and clippe theyr berdes, and poll theyr hedes, and so make them honest agenst Ester day.'

Brand, *Popular Antiquities*, 1849

'The nobles shave their cheeks but let the moustache grow freely so that it covers the mouth.'

Diodorus Siculus, *Description of the Celts*, first century BC

'No person or persons, the king's subjects within this land . . . shall be shorn or shaven above the ears, or use the wearing of hair upon their heads, like unto long locks called "glives", or have or use any hair growing upon their upper lip, called or named a "cronmeal".'

Henry VIII, 'Prohibition of Gaelic Dress in Ireland', 1537

Set a pail of water outside a door or window last thing at night to catch the reflection of the first rays of the sun dancing with delight at the Resurrection

'*Gwyl* , the Welsh for "festival", is simply the Latin *vigilia*, "a watch". Originally it meant the vigil or watch that was kept the evening of a night preceding a Holy Day.'

Revd John Fisher, *The Welsh Calendar*, 1895

'"*Aidche Sathairn*": this phrase is commonly, but wrongly, translated by "Saturday night", while it always means "the eve of Saturday" i.e. "Friday night". Cf. *aidche Domhnaig; aidche Lúain*. The use of *aidche* or *adaig* is perhaps a remnant of the old Celtic custom of making the day follow the night, of which Caesar, *Bell. Gall.* vi, 18, speaks: "*dies natales et mensium et annorum initia sic observant ut noctem dies subsequatur*".'

The Vision of Mac Conglinne, Irish, fourteenth century, edited by Kuno Meyer, 1892

Pasche (pace-egg day)

No eggs were eaten during Lent, so that at Easter there would be more than enough for a feast. The Easter dinner was once as important as that at Christmas. In Anglesey 'decent celebrations' were held 'with dinner, eggs, Lamb or Kidd, even ye poorest family'. The day marked the end of a long period of fasting and self-denial. Fresh meat was often eaten for the first time since the onset of winter.

Unless Easter is very early it is pleasant to be outside: bonfires would be lit and games played over the holiday.

Saint Patrick lit his Easter fire on Slane Hill, within sight of the astonished court of Tara: the Druids had foretold the advent of strangers, but none were prepared for the temerity of the Saint who told them that the flame he had lit in Erin would never be quenched.

'An egg with two yolks means there will be twins in the family soon.'

Irish saying

Tart an earraigh (the thirst of Spring)

To restore golden tints to your hair
'Infuse the bark of rhubarb in wine and wash
your head therewith. Dry with a cloth, and then
by the fire, or in the sun if it be warm. Do this
again and often and the more beautiful will
the hair become, and that without injury to
your hair.'

Meddygon Myddfai, Welsh, thirteenth century

According to Strabo (late first century BC and
early first century AD) the hair of the Celts
'is not only naturally blond, but they use
artificial means to increase this natural quality of the colour – by rinsing their locks
with limewash'.

**Provide your guest with
an umbrella, in case**

'Flurry was to drive us to the races at one o'clock, and we walked to Tory Cottage
by the short cut over the hill, in the sunny beauty of an April morning. Up to the
present the weather had kept me in a more or less apologetic condition: anyone who
has entertained a guest in the country knows the unjust weight of responsibility
that rests on the shoulders of the host in the matter of climate, and Leigh Kelway,
after two drenchings, had become sarcastically resigned to what I felt he regarded
as my mismanagement.'

Somerville and Ross, 'Lisheen Races, Second-hand', *Some Experiences of an Irish R. M.*, 1899

'The soft morrow ande The lustee Aperill,
The wynter set, the stormys in exill,
Quhen that the brycht & fresch illumynare
Uprisith arly in his fyre chare.'

Lancelot of the Laik, Scottish, late fifteenth century

Strong liquors giveth, and they taketh away

The Irish are very prone to colds, because of the watery state of the country: 'for remedy thereof they use an ordinary drink of *aqua vitae*, so qualified in the making that it drieth more and inflameth less than other hot confections.'

Edmund Campion, *History of Ireland*, 1569

'Last night like a fool I drank strong tea and in consequence I tossed from side to side the livelong night and never closed my eyes till five o'clock this morning, with the additional comfort of being in a frantic state of energy.'

Revd Francis Kilvert, *Diary*, 15 April 1871

On the night of 15 and 16 April 1941, a Luftwaffe raid on Belfast killed perhaps a thousand people

'My home town
Has just bin
Blown up:

Dead feet in dead faces,
Corpses still alight,
Students helping kids
And old people out of

Still burning houses.

I have nothing to write
Poems about.

This is my twentieth-century

Night-life.'

Patrick Joseph O'Connor (Padraic Fiacc), born Belfast, 15 April 1924, 'Der Bomben Poet, Spring Song 1941'

'Deep with the first dead lies London's daughter,
Robed in the long friends,
The grains beyond age, the dark veins of her mother,
Secret by the unmourning water
Of the riding Thames.
After the first death, there is no other.'

From Dylan Thomas, 'A Refusal to Mourn the Death, by Fire, of a Child in London'

April

As the leaves begin to shoot to the surface, cut water-lily roots to make dye, or to eat

'Clean and break up the long roots (called in Glendale *Gucagan Báite*) and boil them with a little copperas or alum. Strain and boil the wool in the juice to make a splendid black. The root must be boiled a long time – several hours. "Many a time I saw my mother knit the stockings first and then dye them in the juice." A special raft was made to go out on the lochs to gather the roots, which are always in treacherous mud and difficult to lift.'

Recipes for the Dyeing of Wool

The fleshy root of the plant was also eaten as a delicacy, and the leaves can be used for healing wounds and abscesses.

Mick the Miller, the famous racing greyhound, ran his first race at Shelbourne Park track in the docklands of Dublin on the 18 April 1928 and won

'Bran and Sceolaun, Finn Mac Cumhal's hounds were of a strange breed, for Tyren, sister to Murna, the mother of Finn, had been changed into a hound by the enchantment of a woman of the Fairy Folk, who loved Tyren's husband Ullan; and the two hounds of Finn were the children of Tyren, born to her in that shape. Of all hounds in Ireland they were the best, and Finn loved them much, so that it was said that he wept but twice in his life, and once was for the death of Bran.'

T. W. Rolleston, *The High Deeds of Finn*, 1910

Sir William Robert Wills Wilde was born in 1815 in Castlerea, County Roscommon, and died on this day in 1876

Sir William was a surgeon, husband of Speranza and father of Oscar, and acted as medical commissioner for the Irish census for 1841 and 1851, for which work he was knighted. He also lectured and published extensively in the field of folklore, history and antiquities of Ireland.

'I believe that these Tuatha-de-Dananns . . . were the builders of the great stone Cahirs, Duns, Cashels and Caves in Ireland; while their predecessors constructed the earthen works, the raths, circles and forts that diversify the fields of Erin . . . Within the interior and around these tombs were carved, on unhewn stones, certain archaic markings, spires, volutes, convolutes, lozenge-shaped devices, straight, zigzag and carved lines, and incised indentations, and a variety of other insignia, which, although not expressing language, were symbolical, and had an occult meaning known only to the initiated.'

Sir William Wilde, *Address to the Anthropological Society of the British Association*, Belfast, 1874

Greenness

'Better snow than no rain-storm, when the seed is in the ground.'
[Sowing is better done when snow is out of season, in late April.]

Edward Dwelly, *The Illustrated Gaelic Dictionary*, 1911

'Who would have thought my shrivelled heart
Could have recovered greenness? It was gone
Quite underground – as flowers depart
To see their mother-root when they have blown,
Where they together
All the hard weather,
Dead to the world, keep house unknown.'

George Herbert, poet and divine, born this day in Montgomeryshire, 1593

April

21
The Pleiades are in the constellation of Taurus from 21 April to 21 May

'The Welsh name the seven stars *Seren y gogledd*; the stars of the North and the Pleiades *y faith Seren*.'
'Irish call the Pleiades *drithlana* – sparkling stars, *truidean* – flock of birds, and *cearcean* – hen and chickens.'

Charles Vallancey (1721–1812), *Collectanea de Rebus Hibernicis*

In Taurus it is advantageous to converse on business with a person of influence; they who shall be born are likely to live; he who takes to his bed shall quickly be healed. The sun's intercalary day.
Apostle: Jacobi
Ruler: Mercury

Medieval Irish Zodiac, Basle Library

'There was an especial bull in the bawn of Aillill, and he was the calf of one of Medb's cows, and Finnbennach (the White-Horned) was his name. But he, deeming it no honour to be in a woman's possession, had left and gone over to the herd of the king. And it was the same to Medb as if she had not owned a pennyworth, forasmuch as she had not a bull of his size amongst her cattle.'

'The Cattle-raid of Cooley', Irish, *c.* eighth century

22
The beginning of hawthorn month

Also called whitethorn and may, the hawthorn is an unlucky tree.

'The favourite camp and resting place of the *sidhe* is under a hawthorn tree, and a peasant would die sooner than cut down one of the ancient hawthorns sacred to the fairies.'

Lady Wilde, *Ancient Legends of Ireland*, 1888

'The preparations for the May Day sports and ceremonial in Dublin commenced about the middle of April. For weeks before, a parcel of idle scamps devoted themselves to the task of collecting for the May, and parties, sometimes escorted by musicians, went from house to house to collect materials to adorn the May bush . . . Much as people venerated, at other seasons, their indigenous thorns, especially when growing on the ancient raths, they paid no respect to the sanctity of their character if marked for the May bush.'

Sir William Wilde, *Irish Popular Superstitions*, 1852

1014, Battle of Clontarf

Victory for the Irish high-king Brian
Boru over the King of Leinster and the
allied Norsemen of Dublin, the Orkneys,
Iceland and Man.

'Earl Sigurd arrived at Dublin with all
his army on Palm Sunday. Brodir and
his forces were already there. Brodir
tried to learn by means of sorcery how
the battle would go; the answer he got
was this, that if the battle took place on
Good Friday, King Brian would win the
victory but lose his life, and that if the
battle took place earlier, all Brian's
opponents would lose their lives. Then
Brodir said that they should not join
battle before Friday.

King Brian did not wish to wield weapons on Good Friday; so a wall of shields
was formed round him, and his army was drawn up in front of it.'

Njal's Saga, Icelandic, thirteenth century, translated by Magnus Magnusson and Hermann Palsson

Wear an Easter lily in your buttonhole

'Lilium longiflora is under the domination of the Moon, and by antipathy to Mars
expels poison.'

Nicholas Culpeper (1616–1654), herbalist and astrologer

'To make a capital plaster to cover burns and scalds: take the root of the white lily
and boil it. Reduce it to a pulp and mix with oil and the white of egg, spreading it on
lint. The oftener this is applied the better.'

Meddygon Myddfai, Welsh, thirteenth century

'Hair should be cut when the moon is waxing: snip a little for luck.'
'Peats should be dug when the moon is waning or they will never dry out.'

Skye superstitions

Spring makes a young man's thoughts turn to love and marriage

'Dear God! were I fisher and
Back in Binédar,*
And Nelly a fish who
Would swim in the bay there,
I would privately set there
My net there to catch her,
In Erin no maiden
Is able to match her.

We may be, O maiden,
Whom none may disparage;
Some morning a'hearing
The sweet mass of marriage,
But if fate be against us,
To rend us and push us,
I shall mourn as the blackbird
At eve in the bushes.'

[* the Hill of Howth]

From *Nelly of the Top Knots*, translated by Douglas Hyde, 1893

Ramsons or wild garlic (Welsh, *craf y Geifr*) banish both colic and the common cold

'Now for treatment of the Colic and the Iliac
passion: in which disorder we affirm garlic to be
that windy food which advantages the most;
seeing that it generates not thirst, and is most
comfortable.'

Medical tract, Irish, fifteenth century, B.L. Harleian 546

John Ray, on his botanical itinerary through
Wales in 1662, wrote that Ramsey Island, off the
Pembrokeshire coast, was given its name because
of the abundance of ramsons growing there.

The root is very good in salads, giving an almost
delicate taste of garlic. It is also antiseptic,
antiviral, diaphoretic, anthelmintic, expectorant
and hypotensive.

For bleeding of the nose

'Take an old linen cloth and wet it thoroughly in red wine vinegar, or if you have not that, then in any vinegar, burn the linen and apply the powder, blowing it up through a quill; it will restrain the bleeding quickly.'

Meddygon Myddfai, Welsh, thirteenth century

This physician also recommends plugging the nostrils with pounded nettles to stop the nose-bleed.

Mary (patting his head): 'Be quiet, your reverence. What is it ails you, with your wrigglings now? Is it choking maybe?' (She puts her hand under the sack, and feels his mouth, patting him on the back.) 'It's only letting on you are, holy father, for your nose is blowing back and forward as easy as an east wind on an April day . . .'

J. M. Synge, *The Tinker's Wedding*, 1908

In Scotland and the North of Ireland look out for the burgeoning of the bog-violet (*Pinguicula vulgaris*, Latin; *mothan*, Scottish Gaelic; *leith uisce*, Irish)

'The mothan is one of the most prized plants in the occult science of the people as a love-philtre.'

Alexander Carmichael, *Carmina Gadelica*, 1900

'The woman who gives it goes upon her left knee and plucks nine roots of the plant and knots them together, forming them into a "cuach" or ring. It is placed on the mouth of a girl to make the man who kisses her her bondsman.

If a man makes a miraculous escape, it is said of him that he "drank the milk of the guileless cow that ate the mothan."'

Edward Dwelly, *The Illustrated Gaelic Dictionary*, 1911

' 'Tis wondered yet all Thomond round
How brimstone Bet a husband found
But she to me in secret told
That Planksty fair her mate so bold
was booked at once though strong and hale
By boggy roots infused in ale.'

Brian Merriman (*c.* 1747–1805), 'The Midnight Court'

April

29 Watercress is a spring tonic: it will disperse melancholy and cast out worms and blackheads

Watercress sauce is good with fish dishes: separate the stalks and leaves of a bunch of cress, boil the stalks (with a fish head) to make a stock. Melt the butter with the flour and add the stock. When the sauce has thickened add the chopped leaves and seasoning.

'Though goodly ye deem the salt meat and the fresh
that are eaten in banqueting houses,
I had liefer eat a tuft of fresh watercress
in some place without sorrow.'
'The Madness of Sweeney', Irish, ninth century

'Cresses green culled beneath a stone,
and given to a woman in secret.
The shank of the deer in the head of the herring,
and in the slender tail of the speckled salmon.'
Alexander Carmichael, *Carmina Gadelica*, 1900

30 To a birch tree cut down, and set up in Llanidloes for a maypole

'No more will the birds sleep, no more
will they sing in their shrill note
on your fair gentle crest, sister of
the dusky wood, so incessant
will be the hubbub of the people
around your tent – a cruel
maiming!'
Gruffydd ab Addaf ap Dafydd (*c.* 1340–*c.* 1370)

'This evening being May Eve I
ought to have put some birch and
wittan (mountain ash) over the
door to help keep out the "old
witch". But I was too lazy to go out
and get it. Let us hope the old witch
will not come in during the night.
The young witches are welcome.'
Revd Francis Kilvert, *Diary*, 30 April 1870

MAY
Beltane and dairy month

Breton: *Mae* Cornish: *Miz Me*
Irish: *Bealtaine* Manx: *Boaldyn*
Scottish: *Maigh* Welsh: *Mai*

May

La buidhe Bealltuinn (Gaelic: the yellow day of Beltane)
Calan Haf (Welsh: the first day of summer)

'On the first of May the herds[men] of every village hold their Beltein . . . They make a fire of wood, on which they dress a large caudle of eggs, butter, oatmeal and milk; and bring . . . plenty of beer and whiskey, for each of the company must contribute something. The rites begin with spilling some of the caudle on the ground, by way of libation; on that every one takes a cake of oatmeal, upon which are raised nine square knobs, each dedicated to some particular being, the supposed preserver of their flocks and herds, or to some particular animal, the real destroyer of them; each person then turns his face to the fire, breaks off a knob, and flinging it over his shoulder, says "This I give to thee, preserve thou my horses; this to thee, preserve thou my sheep" and so on. After that they use the same ceremony to the noxious animals. "This I give to thee, O fox! spare thou my lambs; this to thee, O hooded-crow! and this to thee, O eagle!"'

Thomas Pennant, *A Tour in Scotland and Voyage to the Hebrides*, 1772

Washing your face in dew gathered before dawn, particularly from a hawthorn bush or ivy leaves, will make you beautiful; churning at sunrise will ensure a good season of dairying.

The second day of Beltane; a good time to visit holy healing wells

Wells throughout the Celtic lands were visited at Beltane, or on the first Sunday in May. The water is best drunk or washed in at sunrise, and in Gaelic Scotland and

Ireland may be most effective if drunk from a spoon or cup made from the horn of a living cow.

Before using the water, be sure to throw in a silver coin, pin or other suitable offering; insulting the well by leaving rubbish may cause it to dry up or move away. After drinking, tie a rag torn from your clothing to a nearby bush; anyone who dares to remove such offerings will take your troubles or sickness with them.

Some wells were useful for simply providing water, though in an unorthodox way. Gerald of Wales (Giraldus Cambrensis) reports on a well in Munster and another in Brittany which cause heavy rainfall if the pilgrim visits or even looks at them, although the sky may have been clear beforehand.

Unlucky Cross-mass or Avoiding Day

In the Church's calendar this is the feast of the Finding of the Holy Cross by St Helena on 3 May 326. But Highlanders persisted in believing it outstandingly unlucky, because it was also the day when the rebel angels were 'avoided' out of Heaven and fell to earth. No task begun today will ever be finished, and the very day of the week on which it falls will be ill-omened throughout the year.

Ill-luck to cattle can be avoided by placing rowan-wood crosses tied with red thread over their byres, or by squirting a little milk from each udder onto the earth today.

'The great Sabbats of the Forfarshire witches were held four times a year at Candlemas, Roodday, Lammas and Halloween. In the Aberdeen area, Roodday and All Halloweve witnessed the great Conventions. Witches convened upon the Roodday early in the morning upon Saint Katherine's Hill at the head of Andrew Gowis close.'

J. M. McPherson, *Primitive Beliefs in the North-East of Scotland*, 1929

May-flowers now in bloom

Many plants are locally called 'May flowers', including lady's smock, stitchwort, lily of the valley and even primroses in Shetland, as well as the blossoms of the magic may-tree or hawthorn. But in Ireland and parts of Wales, the classic May-flower is the showy marsh marigold, *Caltha palustris*, 'Mary's golden flower of the marsh', the Welsh *Gold y Gors* and the Irish *Beárnán Bealtaine*, 'Beltane shrub'.

In Ireland, bunches of this May-flower were hung over doors and around wells at Beltane; in mid-Wales they were gathered before May-day dawn and strewn on cottage paths. On no account, however, must this or any other May-flower be brought into the house before 1 May, and some say not even then.

May

5

Take care of your health at this season of changeable weather

'In this month do not eat sheep's heads or trotters. Use warm drinks and take gentle emetics. Drink cold whey, and the juice of fennel and wormwood.'

Meddygon Myddfai, Welsh, thirteenth century

'It is also considered very dangerous to sleep in the open air on May-day, or at any time during the month of May. Several of the diseases to which the Irish peasantry are liable are attributed to "sleeping out".'

Sir William Wilde, *Irish Popular Superstitions*, 1852

'May showers make milk and meal.'
'Water in May, bread all the year.'
'Better is snow in May than to be without rain.'

Highland proverbs

6

Babies born now 'between the Beltanes', have 'skill of man and beast'

Others, like the child searched for in this song, must beware of being led astray by fairies.

'I searched the hill from end to end,
      from side to side
I did not find my Cùbhrachan.
I found the track of the brown otter
I did not find my Cùbhrachan.
I found the track of the
      swimming swan
I did not find my Cùbhrachan.
I found the track of the duck on
      the pool

I did not find my Cùbhrachan.
I found the track of the spotted fawn
I did not find my Cùbhrachan.
I found the track of the cow in the bog
I did not find my Cùbhrachan.
I found the track of the mist on the hill
I did not find my Cùbhrachan.'

Hebridean song

Dairying in full swing; beware butter thieves

'The cheese of sheep, the milk of goats and the butter of cows are at the best.'
Book of Iago ab Dewi, Welsh, fourteenth century

'The most efficacious mode of butter-stealing . . . is to follow the milch-cow, as she walks either field, or road, or boreen, and picks up the tracks made in the soft earth by the four feet of the animal, or gather the bits of clauber that stick between the clefts of the feet. Should a set of these be thus acquired, the farmer may expect but a poor return of butter for the next twelve months: but if procured by the owner of the beast she is henceforth invulnerable.'
Sir William Wilde, *Irish Popular Superstitions*, 1852

'If anyone comes to ask them [the Irish] for fire during the month of May, they not only refuse it, but drive him out of doors with curses, imagining this to be an omen that their butter will be stolen all summer long.'
F. M. Mission, *Memoirs and Observations on his Travels through England*, 1719

Furry Dance Day at Helston, Cornwall

'At Helston, a genteel and populous borough town in Cornwall, it is customary to devote the 8th of May to revelry . . . It is called Furry Day, supposed Flora's Day. In the morning, very early, some troublesome rogues go round the streets with drums, or other noisy instruments, disturbing their sober neighbours: if they find any person at work, they make him ride on a pole, carried on men's shoulders, to the river.

In the afternoon the gentility go to some farm-house in the neighbourhood to drink tea, syllabub etc., and return in a Morris-dance to the town, where they dance through the streets till it is dark, claiming a right to go through any person's house, in at one door and out the other.'
The Gentleman's Magazine, 1790

The Furry Dance Song

'Robin Hood and Little John, they are both gone to Fair-O
And we will to the merry greenwood, to see what they do there-O.
And for to chase-O, to chase the buck and doe
Hal-an-Tow, jolly Rumbelow
And we were up, as soon as any day-O
And for to fetch the Summer home
The Summer and the May-O
For Summer is a-come-O
And Winter is a go-O.'

May

9 The traditional date for calving in Wales; wild cherry in blossom

'A certain knight, named Gilbert Hagurnell, after a long and unremitting anguish lasting three years, and the most extreme pains as of a woman in labour, at length gave birth to a calf. This event was witnessed by a great company of onlookers. Perhaps it was a portent of some extraordinary calamity yet to come. But more probably it was the punishment exacted for some unnatural vice.'

Gerald of Wales, *Journey through Wales*, 1188

'Monday the 9th May, 1870. Now the various tints of green mount one over another in the hanging woods of Penllan above the dingle . . . The grass was jewelled with cowslips and orchises. The dingle was lighted here and there with wild cherry, bird cherry, the Welsh name of which being interpreted is "the tree on which the devil hung his mother".'

Revd Francis Kilvert, *Diary*, 9 May 1870

10 Marry in May, rue for aye

May marriages are very unlucky. Welsh medieval law laid down detailed rules for the division of property if marriage broke down within seven years.

'It belongs to the woman to divide and to the man to choose. The pigs for the man and the sheep for the woman: if there are sheep and goats, the sheep for the man and the goats for the woman. Of the sons, two thirds to the father and one to the mother: the eldest and the youngest to the father, and the middle to the mother.

All the milk vessels, except one pail, to the woman; all the dishes, except one dish, to the woman; all the vessels for drink to the man. The bedclothes which are over them to the woman, and those which are under them to the man until he takes a [new] wife. After he takes a wife they belong to the woman, and if the [new] wife who comes to the man sleeps on them, let her pay the woman from whom he separated a wyneberth [shame-fine].'

The Laws of Hywel Dda, Welsh, early medieval

The feast of St Comgall and St Asaph

St Comgall of Bangor (517–603) was one of the most militantly ascetic of Irish saints. Ordained after an early career as a soldier, he founded the monastery of Bangor by Belfast Lough in Ulster, where his many followers were subject to rigid discipline and permitted only one small meal a day. From this training camp for Christian commandos, missionaries like St Columbanus and St Gall journeyed to Italy, Switzerland and Scotland.

The Rule of St Comgall

'This is the most important part of the Rule;
love Christ, hate wealth.
Devotion to the King of the sun
and kindness to people.

If anyone begins the path of repentance
It is sufficient to advance a step every day
Do not wish to be like a charioteer.'

St Asaph was a sixth-century Welshman noted for his charm of manners, grace of body, holiness of heart and witness of miracles. He is founder patron of St Asaph (Llanelwy) Cathedral, mother-church of north-east Wales.

May-eve, Old Style

Take precautions against calendar-conservative fairies; a second chance to try Beltane divinations.

Though rowan is the universally favoured protective plant throughout the Celtic lands, in parts of Wales vervain was preferred, and May-eve was called *Cynnull y Ferfaen* ('Gather the Vervain'). One of the Nine Powerful Herbs, a vervain garland hung around the neck will also ward off nightmares.

Women who wish to dream of their future husbands should go 'after sunset on May Eve, to a bank on which the yarrow grows plentifully, and gather therefrom nine sprigs of the plant, repeating:

"Good morrow, good morrow, fair yarrow
And thrice good morrow to thee
Come tell me before to-morrow
Who my true love shall be."

The yarrow is brought home, put into the right-foot stocking, placed under the pillow, and the mystic dream is confidently expected. But if the girl opens her lips to speak after she has pulled the yarrow, the charm is broken.'

Sir William Wilde, *Irish Popular Superstitions*, 1852

The pardon of Gelvest the Little, protector of young crops against the cold of winter and the white frosts of early spring

'His oratory in the mountains of Arrée, near the forest of Duault, was until recently celebrated for a warlike procession held after Vespers on the eve of the Festival. Pilgrims brandished clubs of holly or oak, iron-headed and fastened to the wrist by a thong. Everyone waits for Vespers ranged in two camps. When the bell sounds the people stream into church in which stands the little figure of the saint. Magnificat intoned, the clubs of the congregation raised and one party cries:

"Throw off the frost, throw off the frost,

Oats and wheat to the Cornouaillais."

The Vannetais (from Vannes) reply;

"Throw off the frost,

Oats and wheat and the black corn to the Vannetais!"

The two sides then pick up the banner and the statue on its stretcher and the Rector of Duault, very pale, advances between them. The congregation then goes outside the church and clamour breaks out, men and women shouting, "Scatter the frost!" Great bloodshed, the plaster saint shattered, the victorious side carries off the banner, and the harvest is protected.'

Anatole Le Braz, *The Land of Pardons*, 1906

Cross-mass, Old Style: an unlucky day in the Highlands

'It is notoriously known what in Killin, within Perthshire, fell tragically out with a Yeoman that lived hard by, coming into Company within an Ale-house, where a Seer or Second-sighted Man sat at table. At the Sight of the Intrant Neighbour, the Seer starting, rose to go out of the House; and being asked the Reason for his haste, told that the intrant Man should die within two Days. At which News the named Intrant stabbed the Seer, and was himself executed two Days after for the Fact.'

Revd Robert Kirk, Minister at Aberfoyle, *The Secret Commonwealth*, 1691

15

Ling, or heather, grows on mountains, bogs and heaths

The farmer burns it to provide fresh young shoots for his sheep, bees produce a strong dark honey from the flowers in July and August and Highlanders have for centuries employed it as bedding, thatching, fuel and dyestuff.

'Barr an Fhroaich: gather the tops when they are young and green, when growing in a shady place. Put them in a pot as you would for lichen [a layer of heather tops, a layer of wool, and so on, and as much water as the pot will then hold] and the wool will be dyed a lovely shade of yellow which can be used as the basis for green if combined with indigo.'

Hebridean recipe for the dyeing of wool

16

Sixth-century Saint Brendan of Clonfert, the navigator

'St Brendan and his followers were for seven years upon the ocean, and not one of all the crew suffered any want, nor did injury befall either body or soul of anyone. And this was a wonder indeed, for Brendan had not allowed them to bring any provisions with them, but he told them that God would provide food for them, wherever they might be.'

Lives and Legends of St Brendan the Voyager, edited by Denis O'Donaghue, 1893

In looking for his Promised Land he may have found America. That the Irish were seagoing adventurers is not in doubt: when the first Norse colonizers came to Iceland in AD 870 they found Irish hermits.

The Anglo Saxon Chronicle says that in AD 891: 'Three Scots [i.e. Irish] came to King Alfred, in a boat without oars, from Ireland, whence they had stolen away, because for the love of God they desired to be on pilgrimage, they recked not whither. The boat in which they came was made of two hides and a half; and they took with them provisions for seven days; and about the seventh day they came on shore in Cornwall.'

According to Welsh tradition, the day when Noah entered the Ark

'According to the most ancient histories of the Irish, Cesara, the grand-daughter of Noah, hearing that the Flood was about to take place, decided to flee in a ship with her companions to the farthest isles of the West, where no man had ever yet lived. She hoped that the vengeance of the Flood would not reach to a place where sin had never been committed. All the ships of her Fleet were wrecked, and only hers survived, carrying three men and fifty women. It put in by chance on the Irish coast, one year before the Flood. But in spite of her cleverness and (for a woman) commendable astuteness in seeking to avoid evil, she did not succeed in avoiding the general disaster.'

Gerald of Wales, *The History and Topography of Ireland, c.* 1187

'The Welch are extremely particular in keeping up the history of their genealogy; every Welchman being more or less a herald. It is a sorry Welch pedigree that does not, at least, reach to Noah.'

Francis Grose, *Provincial Glossary*, 1811

Rogation-tide generally falls in May; milkwort or 'rogation flower' blooming

The thirty-seventh, thirty-eighth and thirty-ninth days after Easter are 'Rogation Days', 'asking days', when people walked in procession round their fields to bless the crops and well, and to 'beat the boundaries' of their parish.

In Wales, Cornwall and England, girls going 'processioning' wore garlands of milkwort, whose botanical name (*Polygala vulgaris*) means 'much milk'. Usually deep blue but sometimes white or pink, this flower was believed to be a sign of good dairying pastures, and was also prescribed to increase the milk of nursing mothers. In Wales it is *Llysiau Crist* ('Christ's herb'), but in north-west Ireland it belongs to the fairies, who make soap from its leaves and roots.

Ascension Day and Pardon of Saint Yvo at Tréguier

'St Yvo, the advocate of the poor, was indeed a lawyer, which is rare among saints.
On his feast day the congregation chant: *Advocatus e non latro, Res miranda
populo* – a lawyer and not a thief, a marvel to the people!
Born in 1253 at Kermartin near Tréguier, he was canonized in 1347.
Generally represented with the cat as his symbol, a lawyer who watches for his
prey, darts at it, plays with it and never lets it escape.'
Revd Sabine Baring-Gould, *Lives of the Saints*, 1877

Ascension Day, or 'Holy Thursday', forty days after Easter, is the day when
Christ ascended into Heaven. Any rainwater which falls today comes straight
from a Heaven open to receive him, and will cure many complaints, particularly
eye-troubles.

'Take not thy coat off before Ascension Day.'
Book of Iago ab Dewi, Welsh, fourteenth century

Beware the pishogue curse on your dairy

'Some months ago I was on a visit to some friends in the south of Ireland, and one
morning . . . a servant rushed into the room, screaming hysterically that the
dairymaid had just found pishogue on the dairy floor. Pishogue is a white,
yellowish fungus made at dead of night, after a solemn incantation of the devil,
according to a secret rite which has been handed down from generation to
generation . . . In the cool, trim dairy, upon the post of the door, I saw daubs of
pishogue. My host . . . informed me under his breath that he might expect bad luck
with the dairy, as it was indeed the cursed pishogue. That very evening . . . his
twenty splendid milch cows . . . were absolutely dry, and for months they remained
so, while a tenant who was noticed to give up his weekly attendance at mass, his
dairy stock suddenly took on the appearance of well-fed cattle. Every one knew he
was the man who had put pishogue on his master.'
Knowlson, *A London Journal*, 1909

May

The feast of St Collen; Montrose executed, 1650

St Collen, the patron of Llangollen in Clwyd, saved the people of the town from an evil giantess. He is also associated with Glastonbury.

James Graham, Marquis of Montrose (1612–1650) led his army of Highlanders and Irishmen to victory after victory over the Scots Covenanting enemies of King Charles I. Finally betrayed, he was hanged on a thirty-foot gibbet at Edinburgh Market Cross; he went to his death 'like a bridegroom', with even one of the hangmen in tears.

'He either fears his fate too much
Or his deserts too small
That dares not put it to the touch
To gain or lose it all.'
Attributed to Montrose

Gemini

In Gemini he who falls into bonds shall speedily be loosed; they that shall be born are likely to live; he who taketh to his bed is quickly healed and his arms will specially suffer.
Apostle: Thomas
Ruler: Saturn
Medieval Irish Zodiac, Basle Library

'"But how to save you, Tamlane?" quoth Burd Janet.
"You must spring upon me suddenly, and I will fall to the ground. Then seize me quick, and whatever change befall me, for they will exercise all their magic on me, cling hold to me till they turn me into red-hot iron. Then cast me into this pool and I will be turned back into a mother-naked man. Cast then your green mantle over me, and I shall be yours, and be of the world again."'
'Tamlane', Scottish folktale, collected by Joseph Jacobs

Collect the magical broom flowers for love-charms, but beware the Being in the Broom, the plant's fairy guardian

'But when ye gang to Broomfield Hill
Walk nine times round and round
Down a bonny burn bank
Ye'll find your true love sleeping sound.

Take ye the blossom of the broom
The blossom it smells sweet
And strew it at your true-love's head
And likewise at his feet.'

'Broomfield Hill', Scots Border ballad

Broom (*Sarothamnus scoparius*) can also be used for making brushes, but never in May. In this month it is literally fatal to cut, buy, or use a new broom.

'Sweep with a broom that is cut in May
You'll sweep the head of the house away.'

Scottish saying

Protect your dairy from witches and other malevolent creatures

'If the good housewife perceives the effect of the malicious on any of her kine, she takes as much milk as she can drain from the enchanted herd, for the witch commonly leaves very little. She then boils it with certain herbs, and adds to them flints and untempered steel: after she secures the door, and invokes the three sacred persons. This puts the witch into such an agony, that she comes nilling-willing to the house, begs to be admitted, to obtain relief by touching the powerful pot: the good woman then makes her terms; the witch restores the milk to the cattle and in return is freed from her pains.'

Thomas Pennant, *A Tour in Scotland and Voyage to the Hebrides*, 1772

Celtic farmers were careful to leave a bowl of clean water, new milk or beer outside each night for the 'Good People'. Elves, Brownies, Manx Bugganes and Scottish Trows were notoriously spiteful creatures. If neglected, they exacted revenge by casting an evil eye on the herd, bringing bitter milk, or no milk at all.

Milking Song

'Bless, O God, my little cow,
Bless, O God, my desire,
Bless Thou my partnership
And the milking of my hands, O God.
Bless, O God, each teat.
Bless, O God, each finger;
Bless Thou each drop
That goes into my pitcher, O God.'

The feast of St Dunchadh of Iona (d. 717), a patron of ships and fishermen; gather carrageen moss

Carrageen or cairgein 'moss' (*Chondrus crispus*) is, in fact, a seaweed. It should be gathered at the 'spring' tides, for it can be found only at very low water. Spread it on clean grass to be washed by rain and bleached by the sun, until it turns from a dark purple to white with pink edges. When dried, take a handful, wash in cold water and put it into a quart pan of milk; bring to the boil and then simmer gently for twenty minutes. Strain and stand the bowl in a cool place until set; then add a little sugar if desired. It is eaten with cream or slightly turned milk. It is a most nourishing diet for invalids and those recovering from fevers.

Recipe from South Uist, Hebrides

Whitsunday often falls in late May

Whitsunday celebrates the descent of the Holy Spirit upon the assembled disciples in the form of tongues of fire. Also called Pentecost (Greek *pentekosti*, 'fiftieth day', whence the Gaelic *Caingis*) it is a movable feast, occurring fifty days after Easter. Its Welsh and English names – *Sulgwyn*, 'White Sunday' – refer to the white robes worn by the converts traditionally baptized at this season of general rejoicing.

'For the Whitsun church-ale two young men of the parish are yerely chosen to be warders . . . who make a collection among the parishioners of whatsoever provision it pleaseth them voluntarily to bestow. This they employ in brewing, baking and other acates against Whitsunday: upon which holydays the neighbours meet at the church house and merrily feed on their own victuals . . . which, by many smalls, groweth to a meetly greatness.'

Carew, *Description of Cornwall*, 1602

The feast of St Melangell, pioneer hunt saboteur

St Melangell (or Monacella) apparently came from Ireland to establish a nunnery at Pennant in the Berwyn hills of northern Powys, Wales. One day a local prince named Brochwel Ysgythrog – 'Brocwel the Tusked' – was hunting a hare which took refuge under St Melangell's skirts. Though he urged on his hounds to the kill, they refused to move – some say because a miraculous thorn hedge sprang up around the saint. The prince then begged her forgiveness and gave her land to build a chapel.

Hares – known locally as *wŷn bach Melangell*, 'Melangell's little lambs' – can still be seen on the medieval screen at Pennant Melangell near Llangynog, where the saint's unique twelfth-century shrine also survives.

High season for butter-making

'At the dairy it was butter morning and Fair Rosamund was making up the sweet rolls of rich golden butter. Mrs Knight says the butter is so golden at this time of year because the cows eat the buttercups. The reason the whey is so sweet and wholesome in May or June is because the grass is so full of flowered and young sweet herbs.'

Revd Francis Kilvert, *Diary*, 28 May 1874

'The Breton wife believes that the best butter is made when the tide has just turned and is beginning to flow, that milk which foams in the churn will go on foaming till the hour of high water is past, and that milk extracted from the cow while the tide is rising will boil up in the pot and overflow the fire.'

Sir James Frazer, *The Golden Bough*, 1890–1915

Oak Apple Day

Today is the birthday of King Charles II and the anniversary of his Restoration to the throne of England in 1660 after the Civil War. In memory of his escape by hiding in an oak after the Battle of Worcester, sprigs of oak leaves – if possible including an 'oak-apple' – were worn on this day, especially in Royalist Cornwall and along the Welsh border.

During the Civil War battle of Braddock Down (1643) in Cornwall, the King's father, Charles I, set up his standard in an oak tree. After his execution in 1649 its leaves suddenly turned white as a symbol of his martyrdom, and remained so until the early eighteenth century.

Ascension Day falls hereabouts in late-Easter years; avoid working

'Yesterday, being Ascension Day, work was entirely suspended at Lord Penrhyn's extensive slate quarries near Bangor. The cessation of work is not due to any religious regard for the day, but is attributed to a superstition, which has long lingered in the district, that if work is continued an accident is inevitable. Some years ago the management succeeded in overcoming this feeling, and in inducing the men to work. But each year there was a serious accident, and now all the men keep at a distance from the quarries on Ascension Day.'

The Times, 1888

Avoid Highlanders on windy days

'The common habit of the Highlander is far from being acceptable to the eye. With
them a small part of the plaid . . . is set in folds and girt round the waist to make of
it a short petticoat that reaches halfway down the thigh: the rest is brought over the
shoulders and fastened before, below the neck often with a fork, and sometimes
with a bodkin or sharpened piece of stick. This dress is called the "quelt", and for
the most part they wear the petticoat so very short that in a windy day, going up a
hill, or stooping, the indecency of it is plainly discovered.'

Edward Burt, *Letters from a Gentleman in the North of Scotland*, 1732

JUNE

the month of Midsummer

Breton: *Even*   Cornish: *Miz Epham* (summer month)
Irish: *Meitheamh*   Manx: *Mean Souree*
Scottish: *And t'Og mhios* (young month)   Welsh: *Mehefin* (Midsumme

A good leak in June sets all in tune

Scottish proverb

June should be warm, but a wet month is good for grass to make hay, that all-important crop in the stock-rearing Celtic lands. Sheep are usually shorn in this month and peat-cutting for winter fuel should be well advanced by now, to allow plenty of time for drying. A lucky month to be born or married in.

'In this month drink a cup of cold water daily, fasting. Drink also warm milk, and eat lettuce. Do not drink ale or mead.'

Meddygon Myddfai, Welsh, thirteenth century

Telling the herring in the Isle of Man

'From June until early October, if the weather continues favourable, the fishing fleet of the Isle of Man, with Cornish and Irish vessels, amounting to about 600 sail, hunt the herring.

A boat has been known to bring in as many as 98,400 herrings, the product of one night's catch. When the fishermen tell their herrings, they add to every hundred (120) three fishes, which they distinguish by the name of warp, and they throw in a single herring, which they call tally – making in the whole 124 fish to the hundred.

The herring is a very delicate fish, and is killed with a very small degree of violence. When taken out of the water it gives a peculiar squeak and instantly expires, hence the proverb "As dead as a herring".'

William Harrison, *Mona Miscellany, c.* 1870

The preparation of 'caller' herring
Remove the head and tail, scrape the scales and clean the fish. Dab a little mustard or horseradish sauce on the herring and roll in seasoned, coarse oatmeal. Fry in oil, or with a little bacon, until brown. Drain on paper and serve with a slice of lemon.

June

The feast of St Kevin of Glendalough, nature-lover

St Kevin (d. 618) was the founder of the famous Irish monastery of Glendalough (the Valley of the Two Lakes), whose extensive remains can still be seen in Wicklow. The many stories about St Kevin reflect his great love of the natural world.

'At one Lenten season, St Kevin, as was his way, fled from the company of men to a certain solitude, and in a little hut that did but keep out the sun and the rain, gave himself earnestly to reading and to prayer, and his leisure to contemplation alone.

And as he knelt in his accustomed fashion, with his hands outstretched through the window and lifted up to heaven, a blackbird settled on it, and busying herself with her nest, laid in it an egg. And so moved was the saint that in all patience and gentleness he remained, neither closing nor withdrawing his hand: but until the young ones were fully hatched he held it out unwearied, shaping it for the purpose.'
Helen Waddell, *Beasts and Saints*, 1934

Feast of St Petroc, the patron saint of Cornwall

Petroc's career well illustrates the close links between the Celtic lands during the sixth-century 'Age of the Saints'. The son of a South Wales prince, he was educated in Ireland, and founded his monastery at Petroc's-stow (now Padstow) in north Cornwall. His last years were spent as a hermit in a beehive hut on Bodmin Moor, and his relic chest still exists in Bodmin church.

The saint is said not only to have cured a poor dragon which came to him with a splinter in its eye, but also to have saved the life of a stag, which took refuge with him from its pursuers, and to have converted the hunter and his attendants.

'Alas for the Red Dragon, for its end is near. Its cavernous dens shall be occupied by the White Dragon, which stands for the Saxons you have invited over. The Red Dragon represents the people of Britain, who will be overrun by the White One.'
Geoffrey of Monmouth, *The Prophecies of Merlin* from *History of the Kings of Britain, c.* 1136

June is a lucky month for weddings

Lady Windermere: 'Windermere and I married for love.'
Duchess of Berwick: 'Yes, we begin like that. It was only Berwick's brutal and incessant threats of suicide that made me accept him at all, and before the year was out, he was running after all kinds of petticoats, every colour, every shape, every material. In fact, before the honeymoon was over, I caught him winking at my maid, a most pretty, respectable girl. I dismissed her at once without a character. No, I remember I passed her on to my sister; poor dear Sir George is so short-sighted, I thought it wouldn't matter. But it did, though – it was most unfortunate.'

Oscar Wilde, *Lady Windermere's Fan*, Act I, 1891

Mr Bumby: 'Good Heavens! How marriage ruins a man! It's as demoralizing as cigarettes, and far more expensive.'

Oscar Wilde, *Lady Windermere's Fan*, Act III, 1891

'A little wife for the big man, a big wife for the little man.'
South Uist proverb

Gather plantain in preparation for Midsummer, or for sore feet

Great plantain (*Plantago major*), also called 'waybreadth', and *Llydan y Ffordd* (Welsh, 'broad one of the road'), grows steadfastly on tracks, paths and lawns, shrugging off damage from feet, wheels and mowers.

'Thou Waybread, mother of worts,
Open from eastward, powerful within,
Over you chariots rolled, over you queens rode,
Over you brides wept, over you bulls bellowed
All these you withstood, all these you confounded.
Withstand now the venom that flies through the air.'

The Lay of the Nine Herbs, ninth century

One of the Nine Midsummer Herbs, this *Slanlus* (Irish, 'healing herb') transfers its self-mending powers to human wounds, burns and sores, including those caused by long walking or ill-fitting shoes. Dip this *Sawdl Crist* (Welsh, 'Christ's heal') in hot water and apply it as a plaster to the inflamed place.

Whitsun falls in early June when Easter is late: morris-dancing rife in eastern Wales

'The dancers are all men; their dress is ornamented with ribbands, and small bells are attached to the knees. The dance is somewhat like that of the Country Bumpkin; and in the course of it, some one of the more active exhibits a kind of somerset [somersault] with the aid of two others. They are attended by Jack and Gill, or as they are called in Wales, the Fool and Megen. The fool is the same as the clown of the old comedy; the megen, a man dressed in women's clothes, with the face smutted to represent a hag. Both entertain the mob by ridiculous tricks; the megen generally solicits contributions from the spectators, and keeps off the crowd by the dread blows of her ladle.'

P. Roberts, *The Cambrian Popular Antiquities*, 1815

'To cross water or to go to sea at Whitsun is very dangerous.'
Welsh saying

St Columba's Eve: try the lamb-luck

On the eve of St Columba's day, the mothers of Highland farming families made a cake of barley, rye or oats, concealing in it a silver coin. It was toasted before a fire of rowan, yew, oak or other holy wood. In the morning the father cut the cake into as many pieces as there were children, all pieces equal. The blindfolded children then drew a piece from the basket in the name of the Father, Son and Holy Ghost. The one who got the coin got the *sealbh uan* ('lamb-luck'), and was given the year's crop of lambs.

No need to take precautions against witches or spirits tonight, for none of these have power at Columba's feast. In the Highlands and Islands, however, St Columba's day was not fixed to the anniversary of the saint's death on 9 June. It was celebrated on the second Thursday in June, Thursday being the day of the week when Columba was born and sacred to him throughout the year.

La Chaluim-Chille: the feast of St Columba, patron of the Highlands and Islands

St Columba, or Colum-cille ('the dove of the church') is among the best loved of the Celtic saints. Born in 521 of an Irish princely family, he is said to have founded 300 monasteries, notably at Derry and Durrow, both sites of holy oak groves (Welsh, *derw*; Irish, *doire*). Perhaps as a penance for provoking a bloody battle over a copyright dispute, he left Ireland as an exiled 'pilgrim for Christ' in 563, establishing the famous island monastery of Iona. Thence he set out on missionary journeys throughout Scotland, converting the King of the Picts and vanquishing an ancestor of the Loch Ness monster. Holy man and poet, prophet, politician and scourge of Druidism, he died on Iona on 9 June 597.

The first day of the oak month

The month which includes Midsummer takes its name from the oak, the most holy, strong and powerful of all European sacred trees. It was revered not only by the Celts, but also by the Greeks and Romans, by the Germanic and Slav peoples and even those of the Middle East.

According to Roman writers, the Celts 'choose groves of oak for the sake of the tree alone, and they never perform any sacred rite unless they have a branch of it. They think that everything that grows on oaks has been sent from heaven by the god himself.'

Pliny the Elder, *Natural History*, first century AD

Such holy oak groves, or *Derunemeton*, were seemingly the preserves of Druids, whose name comes from the Celtic word for 'oak' (*Duir, Deru, Derw, Drui*) and which means either 'oak-knowledge' or just 'the oak-men'.

'Fiercest heat-giver of all timber is green oak, from him none may escape unhurt: by partiality for him the head is set on aching and by his acrid embers the eye is made sore.'

'Death of Fergus', Irish, early sixteenth century, B.L. Egerton MS 1782

June

11
The feast of St Barnabus, patron of peacemakers: sheep-shearing well under way

The Shearing Blessing
'Go shorn and come woolly
Bear the Beltane female lamb,
Be the lovely Bride thee endowing
And the fair Mary thee sustaining,
The fair Mary sustaining thee.

Michael the chief be shielding thee
From the evil dog and from the fox,
From the wolf and from the sly bear
And from the talonned birds of cruel beaks,
From the clawed birds of hooked beaks.'

Alexander Carmichael, *Carmina Gadelica*, 1900

12
St Torannán's Day: try a cure for piles

The Hebridean St Torannán (or Ternan) who crossed the Irish Sea on a stone slab, was a contemporary of Columba. He is one of the Seven Milking Saints who protect Highland cows. His herb is *lus an torranáin*, the figwort, gathered at high tide and set around cattle byres to ensure a good flow of milk.

Figwort (*Scrophularia nodosa*) was also believed to heal 'figs' or piles, an ailment particularly prevalent and distressing during the days of long journeys on horseback. It could alternatively be treated by 'smoking'.

'For piles. Take smoked dried goat's flesh and grind it into as fine a powder as you can. Lay some thereof upon live coals in a fire-proof pan, then put the pan into a chamber-pot and sit thereon.'

Meddygon Myddfai, Welsh, thirteenth century

Birth of W. B. Yeats, Irish poet and visionary, 1865

Innisfree is an island in Lough Gill, County Sligo, where Yeats had long dreamed of living alone in search of wisdom. The poem was written in London in 1890 after the homesick poet was reminded of lake water by a fountain he saw in a shop window display in Fleet Street.

The Lake Isle of Innisfree

'I will arise and go now, and go to Innisfree,
And a small cabin build there, of clay and wattles made:
Nine bean-rows will I have there, a hive for the honey-bee,
And live alone in the bee-loud glade.

And I shall have some peace there, for peace comes dropping slow,
Dropping from the veils of the morning to where the cricket sings;
There midnight's all a glimmer, and noon a purple glow,
And evening full of the linnet's wings.

I will arise and go now, for always night and day
I hear lake water lapping with low sounds by the shore;
While I stand on the roadway, or on the pavements grey,
I hear it in the deep heart's core.'

W. B. Yeats, 1893

Second Sight

'There be odd Solemnities at investing a Man with the Privileges of the whole Mystery of this Second Sight. He must run a Tether of Hair (which bound a Corpse to the Bier) in a Helix about his Middle, from End to End; then bow his Head downwards, and look back through his Legs until he see a Funeral advance till the people cross two Marches [boundaries]; or look back through a Hole where was a knot of Fir. But if the Wind change Points [direction] while the Hair Tether is tied about him, he is in Peril of his Life . . . but some have this Second Sight transmitted ·from Father to Son through the whole Family, without their own Consent or other's teaching, proceeding only from a Bounty of Providence it seems, or by Compact, or by a Complexional Quality of the first Acquirer.'

Revd Robert Kirk, Minister at Aberfoyle, *The Secret Commonwealth*, 1691

'Not only aged men and women have the Second Sight, but also children, horses and cows.'

Francis Grose, *Provincial Glossary*, 1811

June

St Vitus' Day: seek epilepsy cures

St Vitus was a shadowy fourth-century martyr, for whom 'angels danced' while he was in prison. He is thus the patron saint of dancers, actors and late risers, also invoked against 'St Vitus' Dance', epilepsy and other fit-producing ailments. Little understood and much

feared, these 'falling sicknesses' attracted drastic cures.

'In the Scottish Highlands, on the spot where the epileptic first falls, a black cock is buried alive with a lock of the patient's hair and some parings of his nails.'
Arthur Mitchell, *Superstitions of the Highlands . . . relating to lunacy*, 1862

'For falling fits. Burn a goat's horn, directing the smoke upon the patient, and in consequence of the smell he will arise forthwith. Before he has risen, apply dog's gall to his head, and that disease will not attack him any more.'
Meddygon Myddfai, Welsh, thirteenth century

Seek out yarrow, one of the Nine Midsummer Herbs

The common yarrow (*Achillea millefolium*) is a powerful medicinal and magical herb, said to have been used by Achilles (whence its Latin name) to heal wounds made with iron. It will also cure baldness, toothache, dysentery and cystitis and – collected with the right incantation – confer power over men.

'I will pluck the yarrow fair
That more benign shall be my face
That more warm my lips
That more chaste shall be my speech
Be my speech the beams of the sun
Be my lips the sap of the strawberry.

May I be an isle in the sea
May I be a hill on the shore
May I be a star at the waning of the moon
May I be a staff to the weak
Wound can I every man
Wound can no man me.'
Alexander Carmichael, *Carmina Gadelica*, 1900

The feast of St Moling, patron of foxes

St Moling of Ferns (d. 697), Irish abbot and bishop, showed the love of animals
common to many Celtic saints. Among his pets was a fox, which one day stole and
ate a hen belonging to Moling's monks. Abashed by the saint's scolding, the fox
crept away and stole another chicken from a neighbouring nunnery, dropping her
alive at Moling's feet. 'You cannot atone for one theft by another,' said the saint
smiling. 'So take this hen back to the sisters and deliver her to them
unharmed. And in future live without stealing, as other animals do.' To the
wonder of all beholders, the animal carried out his orders exactly.

'No one is bound to pay for the act of a tamed animal: that is
to say, one which has been brought from being a wild
beast to being tame, such as a fawn or a fox.'

The Laws of Hywel Dda, Welsh, early medieval

A Welsh epitaph

'The left leg and part of the thigh of Henry Hughes, Cooper, was cut off and interr'd
here, June 18, 1756.' So reads a miniature tombstone still to be seen at Strata
Florida, Dyfed, Wales, near the grave of the great medieval poet, Daffyd ap
Gwilym. The rest of Henry Hughes, who lost a leg in a coaching accident, later
emigrated to America.

'Where, with my two tried hands, I plied
My trade and, true, in time made good
Though grieving for Pontrhydfendigaid.
Sometimes, all at once, in my tall cups,
I'd cry in *hiraeth* for my remembered thigh
Left by the grand yew in Ystrad Flur's
Bare ground, near the good bard.
Strangers, astonished at my high
Beer-flush, would stare, not guessing,
Above the bar-board, that I, of the starry eye
Had one foot in the grave; thinking me,
No doubt, a drunken dolt in whom a whim
Warmed to madness, not knowing that a tease
Of a Welsh worm was tickling my distant toes.'

From *Lament for a Leg*, John Ormond

June

Cornish cream teas and strawberries now in season

'At St Austell . . . my landlady brought me one of the West Country
tarts, this was the first I met with, though I had asked for them in
many places in Sommerset and Devonshire, its an apple pye with
custard all on the top, its the most acceptable entertainment that
cold be made; they scald their creame and milk in most parts of
these countrys and so its a sort of clouted creame as we call it, with a
little sugar, and so put on top of the apple pye; I was muched pleased
with my supper . . . '

Celia Fiennes, *My Great Journey to Newcastle and to Cornwall*, 1698

'For a dry scurfy disease of the eyelids. Take strawberry juice, hen's fat and May
butter, pound them well together and keep in a horn box. Anoint thine eyelids well
when going to bed, and they will be cured.'

Meddygon Myddfai, Welsh, thirteenth century

'Beer with herbs, a patch of strawberries, delicious abundance . . . '

Irish, tenth century

St Columba's Day, Old Style: a good day to chance upon St John's wort

In the Highlands and Islands, St John's wort (*Hypericum perforatum*) is associated
with the beloved Columba, who always carried it under his left armpit. There, this
Achlasan-Chaluim-Chille ('Columba's armpit package') is most effective if found by
chance, and worn in the same position.

'Armpit package of Columba, kindly
Unsought by me, unlooked for
I shall not be carried away in my sleep
And I shall not be thrust upon iron.'

Alexander Carmichael, *Carmina Gadelica*, 1900

The best known of the Nine Midsummer Herbs, St John's wort was also highly
valued as a powerful 'demon-chaser' by other Celtic peoples, and indeed throughout
Europe. Though called 'Christ's ladder' in Wales, and 'the Virgin Mary's herb' in
Ireland, it was most often dedicated to St John the Baptist, and carefully sought out
on Midsummer Eve or before sunrise on Midsummer Day.

'The virtue of it is thus. If it be put in a man's house, there shall come no wicked
sprite therein.'

Banckes, *Herball*, 1521

The Summer Solstice, when 'Druidic' ceremonies are held at Stonehenge

'Opposite the coast of Celtic Gaul there is an island in the ocean, not smaller than Sicily, lying to the north, which is inhabited by the Hyperboreans, who are so named because they dwell beyond the North Wind. Tradition says that Latona was born there, and for that reason the inhabitants venerate Apollo more than any other god. They are, in manner, his priests, for they daily celebrate him with continual songs of praise and pay him abundant honours. In this island there is a magnificent grove or precinct of Apollo, and a remarkable temple of a round form, adorned with many consecrated gifts. There is also a city sacred to the god, most of the inhabitants of which are harpers, who continually play upon their harps in this temple.'

This description by the Greek geographer, Hecateus of Abdera (fourth century BC), is believed to refer to Britain; the 'remarkable temple' may be Stonehenge or Avebury.

In 1996, specialists in Neolithic archaeology posited that these two great Wiltshire stone monuments may well have been built by Bretons about 2,800–2,600 BC.

Prince Charlie's Gold is visible today

A man named Macrae had the power to put the *fàth-fith*, or spell of invisibility, on anything he desired. He undertook to carry several kegs of gold sent from France to 'Bonnie Prince Charlie' who was then hiding on Skye. On the way, however, he was surprised by Hanoverian soldiers, and fled with his companions down the deep gorge called Fedan Mhor. With his pursuers hard on his heels, he recited the spell and made the kegs immediately invisible, but he himself was taken and executed, so the kegs remain there still. They still reappear for a moment only once a year, precisely at sunrise on 22 June.

'Let me put the *fàth-fith* on you
From dog, from cat
From cow, from horse
From man, from woman
From boy, from girl
From little child
Till I come again.'
Scottish Calendar Customs, 1941

In Cancer they that shall be born are likely to live; he who takes to his bed is cured slowly and his sides mostly suffer; he who takes to flight shall hide in damp places.
Apostle: Bartholomew
Ruler: Jove
Medieval Irish Zodiac, Basle Library

June

Midsummer Eve: divine the identity of your destined partner

'On St John's Eve, the 23rd June, it was formerly held that if an unmarried woman laid upon her parlour table a clean cloth, with bread, cheese and ale, and then sat down as about to eat, the door of her house being left open, the person whom she was afterwards to marry would come into the room and make obeisance to her.'
Scottish Calendar Customs, 1941

'But ye most devilish of all is that of carrying a drawn sword in hand, laying ye scabbard under ye door of ye church and going three times round ye church and pointing the sword towards ye door each time. Ye last time your true love (or ye Devil) will hold the scabbard for you.'
The Life and Works of Lewis Morris (1700–1765), referring to Anglesey, Wales

Midsummer Day; Johnsmass Day; the feast of St John the Baptist

As with all Celtic festivals, celebrations began at midnight of the 'night before the day'.

'I was so fortunate in the summer of 1782 as to have my curiosity gratified by a sight of this ceremony to a very great extent of country. At the house where I was entertained, it was told me that we should see at midnight the most singular sight in Ireland, which was the lighting of Fires in honour of the Sun. Accordingly, exactly at midnight, the Fires began to appear; and taking the advantage of going up to the leads of the house, which had a widely extended view, I saw on a radius of thirty miles, all around, the Fires burning on every eminence which the country afforded. I had farther satisfaction in learning, from an undoubted authority, that the people danced round the Fires, and at the close went through these fires, and made their sons and daughters, together with their cattle, pass through the Fire; and the whole was conducted with religious solemnity.'
The Gentleman's Magazine, 1795

'For every apple seen on St John's Day one hundred will be seen on St Michael's.'
Breton proverb

Seek orpines for divinations and cures

Orpine or 'midsummer men' (*Sedum telephium*) is another of the Nine Midsummer Herbs. Also called 'Livelong', its fleshy leaves allow it to survive long after picking.

'Some used after Midsummer Day is past, to hang it up over their chamber doors, or upon the walls, which will be fresh and green at Christmas . . . with this persuasion, that they that hanged it up, shall feel no disease so long as it abideth green.'

Parkinson, *Theatrum Botanicus*, 1640

Orpines ('heal-all' in northern Ireland) were also used to heal wounds, fevers, sterility and excessive menstrual bleeding.

'Take orpines, bastard balm, small burdock, stinking goose-foot, pimpernel, water avens and the ashes of a stag's horns, boil them in red wine, strain, and drink it daily until it is finished. Being restrained by this potion, the blood will habitually be diverted to the thighs and ankles.'

Meddygon Myddfai, Welsh, thirteenth century

Eat *Cerwr Taliesin* – orpine-leaf salad – in honour of the magician-poet

The historical Taliesin ('beautiful brow') was a sixth-century bard who sang the deeds of King Urien of Rheged, a British champion against the invading Saxons. Welsh legend made him also a magician and shape-changer, a prophet who gained infinite knowledge by tasting the Cauldron of Inspiration.

'I am Taliesin, I sing perfect metre
My original country is the Land of the Summer Stars . . .
I was with my Lord in the highest sphere
When Lucifer fell to the depths of Hell . . .
I have borne a standard before Alexander
I know the names of the stars from north to south . . .
I have been a blue salmon
A dog, a stag, a buck on the mountain
A stock, a spade, an axe in the hand
A stallion, a bull, a roebuck
A grain which grew on the hill
I was reaped and cast in an oven
I have been dead, I have been alive
I am Taliesin.'

Hanes Taliesin, Welsh, thirteenth century

June

Fairies are particularly active at this Midsummer season

'These *Siths* or fairies they call *Sleagh Maith*, or the Good People, it would seem, to prevent the Dint of their ill Attempts (for the Irish use to bless all they fear Harm of) and are said to be of a Middle Nature between Man and Angel, as were Daemons thought to be of old; of intelligent studious Spirits, and light changeable Bodies (like those called Astral) somewhat of the nature of a condensed Cloud, and best seen at Twilight. These Bodies be so pliable through the Subtlety of the Spirits that agitate them, that they can make them appear or disappear at Pleasure.'

Revd Robert Kirk, Minister at Aberfoyle, *The Secret Commonwealth*, 1691

St Peter's Eve: Midsummer's End bonfires in Cornwall

'In Cornwall, the Festive Fires, call'd Bonfires, are kindled on the Eve of St John Baptist, and St Peter's Day, and Midsummer is thence, in the Cornish tongue, call'd Goluan, which signifies both Light and Rejoicing.'

William Borlase, *Observations of the Antiquities . . . of Cornwall*, 1754

'This year, 1881, on the 28th June, the town of Penzance presented a spectacle rarely now seen in Europe. In most of the chief streets, as the summer twilight waned, large bonfires were lighted, and also tar barrels. The Cornish custom of waving torches, i.e. blazing masses of rope dipped in tar and hung from an iron chain, was extensively celebrated. The directors of the fire festival, dressed in hunter's red coats and leathern gauntlets, went among the crowd with squibs and roman candles.'

The Antiquary, 1881

29

The feast day of St Peter, patron of fishermen

'Her fishing dress was clean and neat,
It set me all a-quaking,
I loved her and could almost eat
This maiden ray of Akin;
If ere you saw a cuttle fish,
Her breasts are more inviting,
Like shaking blubbers on a dish,
And tender as a whiting.

Her cheeks are as a mackerel plump,
No mouth of mullet moister,
Her lips of trench would make you
    jump,
They open like an oyster;
Her chin as smooth as river trout,
Her hair as rockfish yellow,
God's Sounds! I view her round about
But never saw her fellow.

But if she frowns I'm gone to pot,
As dead as pickled herring,
The muscles of my heart must rot
And split from clew to earring;
Then in my hammock sink me deep
Within the sight of Hakin,
Then sure she'll melancholy weep
As turtles at their taking.'

From *The Fishing Lass of Hakin*, Lewis Morris
(1700–1765)

'On St Peter's Day the cuckoo goes to
her winter house.'

Highland saying

30

Gather the powerful mugwort between the New and Old Style Midsummers

Mugwort (*Artemesia vulgaris*), called *Llysiau Ifan* (St John's herb) in Welsh, is an ancient magical plant, another of the Nine Midsummer Herbs.

'Una your name is, oldest of herbs
Of might against thirty, or might against three
Of might against venom and flying light
Of might against the vile She who stalks through the land.'

The Lay of the Nine Herbs, ninth century

If this 'Mother of Herbs' is hung over doorways, 'no elves nor no evil thing may come therein'. It can also be used to aid conception, assist childbirth and (boiled with fennel and mint in old ale) to stem hysteria. More prosaically, the crushed leaves of this wayside plant can be sniffed to dispel tiredness, or infused in a bath to soothe sore feet.

'If you would not be weary on a journey, drink in the morning an egg-shell full of the juice of mugwort and garlic, and you will never be hurt nor tired, whatever distance you may walk that day.'

The Book of Ieuan of Sarn, Welsh, medieval

JULY

month of hunger

Breton: *Mezevennik*   Cornish: *Mis Gorephan* (head of the summer mon

Irish: *Iúl*   Manx: *Jerrey Souree* (end of summer)

Scottish: *An Mios buidhe* (yellow month)   Welsh: *Gorffennaf* (completion n

1 Haymaking getting under way

The all-important hay crop, without which livestock could not survive the winter, is generally cut in July. But in years of poor weather, haymaking may be delayed for weeks or even months. Worst of all is a long period of wet weather after the crop has been cut, delaying the mown hay's drying or even rotting it in the field. All sensible farmers therefore carefully observed rain omens in July.

'If the first of July be rainy weather
It will rain, more or less, for four
   months together.'

'Whoever wants a meadow, let him keep it from St Patrick's Day [17 March] until the Winter Calends [1 November]. A meadow is land without use save for hay, with a bank round it. That is why it is kept until the Winter Calends, because it is right to mow it twice in the year. Meadows are forbidden to pigs because they damage the land. He who finds pigs on his meadow, let him take four legal pence [in damages] from their owner.'

The Laws of Hywel Dda, Welsh, early medieval

2 'St Mary's Feast in Summer': the feast of the Visitation of the Virgin Mary to Elizabeth, mother of John the Baptist. Look out for 'Mary's ladder', the centaury

The pretty pink centaury (*Centaurum erythraea*) takes its name from Chiron the centaur-physician, said to have first discovered its virtues as a cure for 'internal stoppages'. Medieval Welsh doctors recommended boiling it with honey and ale as a remedy for heart complaints.

   Centaury is also a holy plant, called *Ysgol Fair* ('Mary's ladder') in Welsh and *Keym Chreest* ('steps of Christ') in Manx, because it grew in his footsteps on the way to Calvary. In Ireland, it will bring a blessing on the house if picked and brought in today. This is likewise a fortunate day for imitating Mary by visiting the mothers of new babies.

The first of the dangerous 'Dog Days'

The hot and unhealthy 'Dog Days', so called because Sirius the Dog Star is in the ascendant, begin today and continue until about 11 August. The sticky, stormy heat of this season provokes plagues and fevers, 'venomous serpents creep, fly and gender', and dogs may become rabid and have to be destroyed. One of the Gaelic names for July, indeed, is *An mìos chrochadh nan Con*, 'the month for hanging dogs'. Hot food and drink, medicinal bleeding, and 'all wanton bed-sports' must be shunned, and fevers treated immediately and drastically.

'For an intermittent fever. Take dandelion and fumitory infused in water, first thing in the morning. Then about noon take wormwood in tepid water, at ten draughts. Eat wheaten bread, oatcakes and young chickens, but no milk foods. If the fever does not end, put the patient in a bath when the fever is on him, and give him an emetic, which will then act more strongly.'

Meddygon Myddfai, Welsh, thirteenth century

Under the ancient Brehon laws of Ireland the owner of a dog which defecates on a neighbour's land has not only to remove the offending article but to present his neighbour with a like quantity of butter in compensation.

Gather magic fern-seed, if you dare

'Go alone to where the ferns grow, with a number of pewter plates – nine or thirteen, I forget which – all laid on top of each other, with a sheet of white paper or linen between the two lower ones. These were held under the fern and when at midnight the seed was dropped so great was its enchanted power that it passed through all the plates except the lowermost two where it got caught on the linen or paper. Then folded up and carried in the pocket of the adventurer who could thereby render himself invisible. And while invisible he could take whatever he wanted.

In Farney they said that all the powers of darkness and evil were mustered to frighten off the temerarious individual while in the act of securing the seed. They could not touch him but yells, screams, thunder whirlwinds, lightnings and the actual appearance of friends all conspired to shake his nerve.'

Article by Enri O'Muirgheasa in *Béaloideas*, 1932

Midsummer Day, Old Style: look out for Snake Stones

'In most parts of Wales, and throughout all Scotland, and in Cornwall, we find it a common opinion of the vulgar, that about Midsummer-Eve (though in time they do not all agree) it is usual for snakes to meet in companies, and that by joyning heads together and hissing, a kind of bubble is formed, which the rest, by continual hissing, blow on till it passes quite through the body, and then it immediately hardens, and resembles a glass-ring, which whoever finds (as some old women are persuaded) shall prosper in all his undertakings. The Rings thus generated, are called *Gleinau Nadroeth*; in English, Snake-Stones. They are small glass Amulets, commonly about half as wide as our finger-rings, but much thicker, and of a green colour usually, though sometime blue, and waved with red and white.'

Letter from Edward Lhwyd, 1701, in Rowland, *Mona Antiqua*

The first railways run in the Isle of Man, 6 July 1873; the fairies leave in disgust

'After the introduction of railways into the island neither Phynodderree nor fairy of any kind has ever been met with by any sober man. It is currently supposed by the Manx people that the shrill, discordant blast of the railway whistle has been more than the delicate aural organs of so sensitive a race as the fairies could stand, and that, disgusted with the inventions of men . . . they have taken their departure from the shores of Mona's Isle for ever.'

E. Callow, *The Phynodderree and Other Legends of the Isle of Man*, 1882

The departure of the Phynodderree must have been a sad loss to Manx farmers. For this strong, long-armed goblin would often help them with the hay harvest, provided he was not offended.

'When badly treated or provoked, Phynodderree could be spiteful . . . An ungrateful farmer found fault with the way Phynodderree had mown his field, saying he could have done it better himself. This enraged Phynodderree, who waited till next year, and when the farmer set to work to mow it he came with a scythe in his hand and chased him off the field. For many years after this the grass remained uncut, everyone being afraid to attempt to mow it.'

E. Callow, *The Phynodderree and Other Legends of the Isle of Man*, 1882

The feast of St Maelruan the Culdee

St Maelruan of Tallaght near Dublin (d. 792) was a leader of the Celtic monks called *Céili Dé* or 'Culdees', meaning 'Servants of God'. Strict vegetarians and teetotallers, they abandoned the restless wanderings of earlier Celtic missionaries and established fixed communities in remote wildernesses – including Iceland and Bardsey Island off north-west Wales.

'Beyond Lleyn there is a small island occupied by extremely devout monks, called the Coelibes or Colidei. Either because of its pure air, which comes across the sea from Ireland, or through some miracle granted because of the merits of the holy men that live there, no one dies in this island except in extreme old age, for disease is almost unheard of. In Welsh the place is called *Ynys Enlli*, in the Saxon tongue, Bardsey Island. The bodies of a vast number of holy men are buried there . . . '

Gerald of Wales, *Journey through Wales*, 1188

The first day of holly month

'Of all the trees that are in the wood
The holly-tree bears the crown.'

So says the Christmas carol, and holly is generally associated with Midwinter and Christmas – when its prickles recall Christ's crown of thorn, and its red berries his sacrificial blood. But holly was sacred to the Romans, the Germanic peoples and the Celts long before the coming of Christianity, and its special month was celebrated, not at the time of its berries, but at that of its much less conspicuous flowers. More significantly, it is also the month just after Midsummer, when the sun is beginning to decline; for the god or king of the evergreen holly (often identified with Bendigeidfran, 'Bran the Blessed' of Celtic mythology) was a guardian of the waning year and the winter, as the oak god ruled the season of growth which culminated at Midsummer.

'Holly, burn it green; holly burn it dry: of all trees whatsoever the critically best is holly.'

'Death of Fergus', Irish, early sixteenth century, B.L. Egerton MS 1782

Remember Bran the Blessed, the holly god, and ravens

'And then Bran the Blessed commanded his head to be struck off. "And take my head", he said, "and carry it to the White Mount in London, and bury its face towards France." And when it was buried, that was one of the Three Happy Concealments of the Island of Britain, and it was one of the Three Unhappy Disclosures when it was dug up, for no plague would ever come across the sea to this Island so long as Bran's head was in that concealment.'

Second Branch of the *Mabinogion*, Welsh, eleventh century, edited by G. and T. Jones

Though Bran's head no longer lies beneath the White Mount – upon which the White Tower of the Tower of London is said to have been built – his guardian birds still haunt the site of his burial. For *Bran* is the Welsh word for crow or raven, and ravens can still be seen at the Tower. If they ever departed – unlikely, since their wings are clipped – London, and perhaps Britain itself, would be overthrown.

The tale of Bran recalls the cult of the severed head, one of the most distinctive and important elements of pre-Christian Celtic religion

'They [the Celts] embalm in cedar oil the heads of their most prominent enemies, preserve them carefully in a chest and display them with pride to visitors, saying that for this head their ancestors, or the owner himself, refused a large sum of money. It is said that some boast that they even refused the weight of the head in gold.'

Diodorus Siculus, *Description of the Celts*, first century BC

After killing the Roman consul Lucius 'they stripped his body, cut off his head, and carried their spoils to the holiest of their shrines. There they cleaned out the head, as is their custom, and gilded the skull, which thereafter served as a holy vessel to pour libations and as a drinking cup for the priest and temple attendants.'

Titus Livius, referring to events in 216 BC

July

Children now restless on hot nights; soothe them with lullabies

Probably the oldest lullaby (or at least child's song) in a Celtic language was for some reason included in a manuscript of otherwise sternly heroic seventh-century verse.

'Dinogad's speckled petticoat
was made from skins of speckled stoat
whip whip whipalong
eight times we'll sing this song.
When your father hunted the land
spear on shoulder, club in hand
thus his speedy dogs he'd teach
Giff Gaff catch her, catch her fetch.
In his coracle he'd slay
fish as lion does his prey.
When your father went to the moor
he'd bring back heads of stag, fawn, boar,
the speckled grouse's head from the mountain
fishes' heads from the falls of Oak Fountain.
Whatever your dad struck with his spear
wild pig, wild cat, fox from his lair
unless it had wings it would never get clear.'

The Book of Aneirin, translated by Gwyn Williams

Gather eyebright and greater celandine for eye remedies

The little, white and yellow eyebright (*Euphrasia officinalis*) of grassy uplands, is a famous eye-curing herb throughout the Celtic lands. In Wales, where it is called *Golwg Crist* ('Christ's sight') or *Ilygad Crist* ('Christ's eye'), eyes were bathed with a distillation of eyebright, fennel and rue; in the Hebrides the herb was used infused in milk.

The bright orange juice of the greater celandine (*Chelodonium majus*) was an equally widespread eye remedy; called 'kill-wart' in Cornwall, it can also be used against skin blemishes.

'For Cloudiness of the eyes. Take the juice of celandine, drop into the eye, and close it as long as a hundred is counted; let this treatment be perseveringly continued.'

Meddygon Myddfai, Welsh, thirteenth century

Death of Anthony Payne, the Cornish giant, 1691

Seven feet six inches tall and massively built, Anthony Payne of Stratton, Cornwall, was the servant and guardian of the Royalist Grenville family during the Civil Wars, and later a Yeoman of the Guard under Charles II. When he died, the floor of his bedroom had to be removed to allow his huge coffin to be brought out.

'Cornineus got great pleasure from wrestling with the giants of Cornwall, of whom there were far more than in any other region of Britain. There was a particularly repulsive one called Gogmagog, who was twelve feet tall, and so strong that he could tear up an oak tree as if it was a hazel wand.'

Geoffrey of Monmouth, *History of the Kings of Britain*, c. 1136

Cornish 'Taking Day' falls about now

'The Cornish maids and men have a custom useful for the encouragement of matrimony. At Crowan, on the Sunday previous to Prayes Crowan fair (July 16th), they go to the parish church, and at the end of the service hasten to Clowance Park, where a large crowd is assembled. Here the young men select their partners for the forthcoming fair; and as sometimes rivals contend for the same beauty, and as sometimes the beauty rejects the generous offer of eager swains, contentions arise, and tussles ensue which afford much amusement to the spectators. "Taking Day" as it is called, is responsible for many happy weddings.'

P. H. Ditchfield, *Old English Customs*, 1896

The Colours of Women

'Fair and foolish, little and loud
Long and lust, black and proud
Fat and merry, lean and sad
Pale and pettish, red and bad
‸igh colour choler shows
‸d she's unwholesome that like sorrel grows
‸ght are the peevish, proud, malicious
‸orst are the red, shrill and jealous.'

‸, *Scottish Proverbs*, 1641

The feast of St Cewydd of the Rain

Hen Gewydd y Glaw, 'Old Cewydd of the Rain', is the south Welsh counterpart of the English St Swithin, whose feast he sometimes shares. If it rains on this day, it will continue to do so for the next forty days. Among the scattered churches dedicated to St Cewydd is Disserth in Radnorshire, where the spirit of a dishonest tanner was exorcised in the eighteenth century.

'Parson Jones summoned the spirit to meet him in Disserth church, and there with three other parsons he faced the spirit, his awed congregation crowding into the churchyard. They saw four parsons enter, armed with books and candles. Presently three of the parsons, paralysed with fear, joined the crowd outside: the devil had blown out their candles. Parson Jones saved his light by hiding it in his top-boot and . . . at last he emerged triumphant, carrying in his hand a silver snuff box, in which he said was the evil spirit . . . reduced to the size of a blue-bottle fly. It was tied to the top of an iron bar and forced into the depths of a quaking mire.'

W. H. Howse, *Disserth*

Foxgloves now blooming: look but leave well alone

The foxglove, *Digitalis purpurea*, 'purple finger plant', is the most striking high summer flower of the Celtic uplands. Its clustered bells are used by foxes to pad their feet for silent hen-stealing raids, and its many other names reveal a still more sinister reputation. *Menyg ellyllon* ('elves' gloves') in Wales; it is *Meuran nan caillich marbha* ('dead women's thimbles') in the Highlands; and *Lus na mban sidhe* ('herb of the fairy women') in Ireland. The 'digitalis' they contain slows the heart muscles, and is still used medicinally; but it is deadly in excess, and could be employed to 'put away' children supposed to be changelings, or make the death-curses of witches doubly sure. White foxgloves, which sometimes occur natural' should be given a particularly wide berth, for they are the special preserve of 't Good People'.

Dog Days continue: look out for rabid dogs

'A guard dog, if it is killed more than nine paces from the door, is not paid for. If it is killed within the nine paces, it is worth twenty-four pence fine. If a dog attacks any person to tear him, and that person kills the dog with a weapon, there is no fine. If a dog bites a person so that blood flows, let the dog's owner pay for the blood: but if the bitten person kills the dog, he will only get sixteen pence. If a notorious dog tears a person on three occasions, it must be killed by the owner: if not, it must be tied to the owner's foot, two spans away from him, and so killed, and let him pay three cows fine to the King. There is no compensation for the evil done by a rabid dog, because no one can control it.'

The Laws of Hywel Dda, Welsh, early medieval

'For the bite of a mad dog. Six ounces of rue, four ounces of garlic, two ounces of Venice treacle and two ounces of pewter filings. Boil for two hours in a closed vessel in two quarts of ale, strain, and give a spoonful fasting each morning.'

Lady Wilde, *Ancient Legends of Ireland*, 1888

Feast of St Thenew, a patroness of single parents

According to her legend, Thenew or Taneu was the daughter of a sixth-century prince of Lothian in southern Scotland. When she was found to be pregnant by a lover of humble birth, her father had her thrown from the summit of Traprain Law; but she floated down gently 'as if she were a bird with feathered wings'. She was therefore set adrift in a leather coracle, but a triumphant procession of fish guarded her until she came ashore at Culross in Fife, where she gave birth by a shepherd's fire. Her baby was St Kentigern or Mungo who became the patron saint of Glasgow.

Gather meadowsweet for its invigorating scent

Meadowsweet (*Filipendula ulmaria*) originally 'mead-sweet', takes its name from its use in flavouring honey-mead drinks.

'It is reported that the flowers boiled in wine and drunk do make the heart merry. The leaves and flowers far excel all other strewing herbs, for to deck up houses, to strew in chambers, halls and banquetting houses in the Summer time: for the smell thereof makes the heart merry, delighteth the senses. Neither does it cause head-ache or loathsomeness to meat, as some other sweet smelling herbs do.'

Gerard, *Herball*, 1597

Also used against fevers and malaria, meadowsweet contains a substance similar to aspirin. In the Highlands it is called *Crios Chú-chulainn*, 'Cuchullain's belt' because the great Ulster hero revived himself by binding it around his waist.

The feast of St Uncumber, helper of those with unwanted lovers

The dubious St Uncumber, also called Wilgefortis or Liberata, was the daughter of the King of Portugal, vowed to virginity. After praying for deliverance from a forced marriage, she miraculously sprouted a large beard, whereupon her suitor fled. She was thus invoked by women who wished to uncumber themselves of unwanted lovers (or husbands).

'Duvenaldus, King of Limerick, had a woman with a beard down to her waist. She also had a crest from her neck down her spine, like a one-year-old foal. In spite of these two enormities, she was not an hermaphrodite, but in other respects was quite normally feminine.'

Gerald of Wales, *The History and Topography of Ireland*, c. 1187

'The Triads of Ireland are a collection of wise sayings made at the end of the ninth century . . . three rude ones of the world: a youngster mocking an old man, a robust person mocking an invalid, a wise man mocking a fool.'

Thomas MacDonagh, *Literature in Ireland*, 1920

Pray to St Margaret, patron of women in childbirth, for deliverance from nurse-kidnapping fairies

'Women are yet alive who tell they were taken away when in Child-bed to nurse Fairy Children, a lingering Veracious Image of them being left in their place (like their Reflection in a Mirror) . . . The Child, and Fire, with Food and other Necessaries, are set before the Nurse as soon as she enters: but she neither perceives any Passage out, nor sees what those People do in other Rooms of the Lodging. When the Child is weaned, the Nurse dies, or is conveyed back, or gets it her choice to stay there . . . The Tramountains [Highlanders] to this Day put Bread, the Bible, or a piece of Iron, in Women's beds when travailling [in childbirth], to save them from thus being stolen.'

Revd Robert Kirk, Minister at Aberfoyle, *The Secret Commonwealth*, 1691

The feast of St Mary Magdalene, patron of penitent women; an unlucky day for Scotland

Mary of Magdala, the follower of Christ to whom he first appeared after his Resurrection, is usually identified with the reformed prostitute who washed his feet with her tears and dried them with her hair.

Her feast was believed unlucky in Scotland, because on this day in 1298 William Wallace's patriot army was routed by King Edward I of England at Falkirk.

'The Scottish nation . . would have fought with the English upon any festival day in the year sooner than upon Magdalene Day, as fearing lest the ill hap which it brought upon them had not been expiated with the reiterated penitential sacrifices of many widow's tears.'

J. Jackson, *The Originall of Unbeliefe*, 1625

Consider toads

'23rd July [in Cornwall]. Mrs H. has two pet toads, which live together in a deep hole in the bottom of a stump of an old tree. She feeds them with bread crumbs, and they make a funny little plaintive squeaking noise when she calls them.'

Revd Francis Kilvert, *Diary*, 23 July 1870

'A young man who lived in this region [Cemais, Dyfed] suffered so much persecution from toads on his sickbed, that it seemed as though all the toads of the entire district had agreed to assemble there. Though a vast number were killed by his friends, yet more kept flocking in. Eventually . . . they stripped a tall tree of branches and hoisted him up into it in a kind of bag. But he was not safe even there . . . for the toads climbed up to look for him, and they killed him and ate him up to the bare bones. His name was Seisyll Esgairhir, which means Longshanks. The judgment of God is never unjust, though it is sometimes hard to understand.'

Gerald of Wales, *Journey through Wales*, 1188

he feast of St Declan, a patron of dogs and back sufferers

St Declan of Ardmore, County Waterford (fifth century), was a precursor and later a companion of St Patrick. Offered taboo dog's flesh disguised as mutton by a pagan chieftain, he instantly restored the cooked dog to life. His shrine was famous for curing back complaints.

'On the 24 July 1826, several thousand persons of all ages and both sexes assembled at Ardmore . . . and commenced their devotional exercises by passing under the holy rock of St Declan. This was not effected without considerable pain and difficulty, owing to the narrowness of the passage, and the sharpness of the rocks. Stretched at full length on the ground on the face and stomach, each devotee moved forward, as if in the act of swimming, and thus squeezed or dragged themselves through. Upwards of 1,100 persons, in a state of half nudity, were observed to undergo the ceremony. A reverend gentleman who stood by . . . was heard to exclaim "O great is their faith".'

Hone, *The Every-day Book*, 1830

25

An excellent day for travelling, being the feast of both St Christopher and St James the Greater

The legendary St Christopher ('Christ-bearer') was a giant who carried the infant Jesus across a dangerous river. He is the chief patron of travellers, and anyone who looks on his image will be preserved from violent death that day.

The Biblical St James the Greater, one of the Twelve Apostles, is the principal guardian of pilgrims, especially those who flocked to his famous shrine at Santiago (St James) de Compostela in northern Spain.

'Get up friend, wake from your accustomed sleep.
Fasten your belt, so that we can get on the road
early, for the day is short and the way is long.'
'Boy, light us a fire quickly, for I am worn out by
the labour of the journey, and by the very long, very
muddy road, full of swamps and foulness.'
'Innkeeper, bring us a pot of ale, or wine, or cider or
mead.'
'O best of girls, give me a kiss.'
From a Latin phrase book for Welsh pilgrims, tenth century

26

The Grand Pardon of St Anne

'A certain young gentlewoman of Auray, who feared dying an old maid, very earnestly begged the saint to grant her a husband; the saint's bounty being equal to her power, she most kindly sent the young lady three several husbands within the space of five short happy years. 'Tis well we have no such shrines in England, or, Heaven bless us! there would be no getting near them.'
Mrs Charles Stothard, *Letters Written during a Tour ... in 1818*

Breton royalist rebels of the 1790s

'It's your salvation that is at stake, Christians! It is your souls that you will save fighting for religion and the King. Saint Anne of Auray herself appeared to me the day before yesterday at half-past two. This is what she said to me just as I'm saying it to you. "You are a priest of Marignay?" "Yes, Madame, ready to serve you." "Well, I am Saint Anne of Auray, God's cousin, once removed. I am still at Auray, although I'm here as well; and I have come so that you may tell the *gars* of Marignay that there is no salvation for them to hope for if they do not take up arms. So you are to refuse them absolution unless they serve God. You shall bless their guns, and *gars* who are free from sin cannot fail to shoot the Blues because their guns will be sanctified!"'
Honoré de Balzac, *The Chouans*, 1829, translated by Marion Ayton Crawford

Battle of Killiecrankie, 1689

On this day an army of Jacobite Highlanders under John Graham of Claverhouse, Viscount Dundee, routed the Lowland Scots supporters of William III of Killiecrankie near Blair Atholl. 'Bonnie Dundee' – reviled by those he persecuted as 'Bloody Clavers' was shot down at the moment of victory. He is said to have been killed by a silver bullet, the one sure weapon against witches and 'Hard Men' charmed against ordinary missiles.

'An Irish battle charm: "O Mary, who had the victory over all women, give me victory over my enemies, that they may fall to the ground, as wheat when it is mown."'

Lady Wilde, *Ancient Legends of Ireland*, 1888

In Leo the messenger who shall arrive is trustworthy; they that shall be born are likely to live; he who takes to his bed is quickly healed and his breast suffers most; he who takes to flight shall get through.
Apostle: Philip
Ruler: Pluto

Medieval Irish Zodiac, Basle Library

The feast of St Sampson of Dol. The Nannau Oak collapsed, 1813

St Sampson of Dol (*c*. 490–*c*. 565) the subject of the earliest biography of a British Celtic saint, was brought up in South Wales. After missionary journey to Cornwall, Ireland and the Channel Islands, he became Bishop of Dol in Brittany, and leader of the British colonists who fled there from the Saxons.

'On the road side [at Nannau near Dolgellau, Gwynedd] is a venerable oak in its last stage of decay, and pierced by age into the form of a Gothic arch; yet its present growth is twenty-seven feet and a half. The very name is classical, Derwen Ceubren yr Ellyll, "the hollow oak, haunt of demons".'

Thomas Pennant, *Tours in Wales*, 1810

According to tradition, this hollow oak was used to conceal the body of Hywel Selau of Nannau, a fifteenth-century gentleman who attempted to assassinate the patriot Owen Glyndwr. But its title suggests a far more ancient significance.

Fraughan, Bilberry or Heights Sunday falls about now

In Ireland, the last Sunday in July – the Sunday before Lammas – is Fraughan Sunday when people flocked to the upland 'Heights' to dance, picnic, and gather fraughans or bilberries (*Vaccinium myrtillis*). These tiny blue-black fruits, also called blaeberries or (along the Welsh borders) wimberries – 'wine berries' – can be made into wine, pies, jam or dyes; but hand picking is a tedious business, and they are best gathered by using a wooden 'wimberry comb' on the low-growing plants. Signalling the end of high summer and the beginning of harvest, this *Fête des Myrtilles* (as it is known in France) was a popular time for courting.

From *The Misty Corrie*

'. . . Your kindly slope, with bilberries and blaeberries, studded with cloudberries that are round headed and red; wild-garlic clusters in the corners of the rock terraces, and abounding tufted crags; the dandelion and pennyroyal, and the soft bog-cotton and sweet-grass there on every part of it, from the lowest level to where the peaks are at the topmost edge.'

Scottish Gaelic, Duncan Bàn MacIntyre (1724–1812)

Hot weather provokes bad temper: beware Irish axemen

'Following the old and evil custom [the Irish] always carry an axe in their hand, as if it were a staff. Because of this, if they wish to do any evil, they can more quickly put the impulse into effect. Wherever they go, they always take this axe with them. When they see the opportunity, or if the occasion to use it presents itself, this weapon does not have to be unsheathed like a sword, or drawn like a bow, or poised like a spear. It can inflict a mortal blow just by being raised a little, without any more preparation. The death-dealing weapon is always ready, and ever at hand – or rather, in their hand.'

Gerald of Wales, *The History and Topography of Ireland, c.* 1187

July

31 Lammas Eve

The end of the hungry Summer months – the last called 'The Bitter Six Weeks', and, most disparagingly, 'July of the Cabbage' – when old potatoes are finished and the new not yet ready for digging. Lammas marks the beginning of harvest.

'Oats being so general a crop in Ireland, one might expect them to be very cheap, but, however, though a great many are grown, there is also a great consumption as all the poor in general eat no sort of bread except that made of oats; and the time of the year when potatoes are out of season (May, June and July) their whole living is oat bread and buttermilk, but so long as potatoes are good they supply the place of bread: therefore oats bear a better price than would be expected, being so general a crop.'

C. Varley, *A New System of Husbandry*, 1770

AUGUST

harvest month

Breton: *Eost*   Cornish: *Est, mis est* (month to harvest)
Irish: *Lughnasa*   Manx: *Luanistyn*
Scottish: *ceud mhios an fhoghair*   Welsh: *Awst*

August

Lá Lughnasa, 'Lewy's fair'

Harvest Games were held in honour of Lugh on his feast day – the memorial of his death – in ancient times in Britain, Ireland and on the continent. Those at Lyons (*Lugdunum*), occupied by the Romans as their Gaulish capitol, were redesignated the Augustus (i.e. the honoured) Caesar's games.

The season of the god Lugh (Welsh *Llew*) the Celtic god of light and genius; he was also called *samhioldanach*, the equally-skilled-in-all-arts, the inventor of *fidchell*, chess.

According to the Irish poet Gofraidh Fionn O'Dálaigh (who died in 1387) he could also leap onto a bubble without bursting it.

The raven was his bird: to dream you see this bird is bad; to see it flying is worse. In Welsh folklore this might denote a bad conscience.

The Sunday of the new potatoes. The first fruits of the wild berries are to be eaten. Hazel month, the wood of the wand of kingship

'Spare the limber tree: burn not the slender hazel.'

'Death of Fergus', Irish, early sixteenth century, B.L. Egerton MS 1782

'He himself went to learn the accomplishments of poetry and science from an ancient sage and Druid named Fenegas, who dwelt on the River Boyne. Here,.in a pool of this river, under boughs of hazel from which dropped the Nuts of Knowledge on the stream, lived Fintan the Salmon of Knowledge, which whoso ate of him would enjoy all the wisdom of the ages.'

T. W. Rolleston, *Celtic Myths and Legends*, 1911

'Three fresh hazelnuts from the finest cluster.'

Lochlainn óg Ó Dálaigh, description of three princes of Thomond, *c.* 1550

Corncrake, of the *Rallidae* family (Latin, *Crex crex*; bean cracker in South Pembroke)

Though shy, this bird can be called by drawing a smooth bone over a serrated one.

Archaeology records the corncrake in Wales in the Holocene period; its habitat is the grassy borders of marshland. In sharp decline since the advent of hay-cutting machinery in the late nineteenth century, it is now only to be found in certain parts of Ireland and the Scottish islands. You will be fortunate to hear its rasping call on a summer's night, and more fortunate still to see one.

'May you sleep like the landrail' [i.e. lie awake all night].
Irish malediction

The eighth Sunday in Trinity falls about now

On Trinity Sundays water sweetened with brown sugar (white will not do) is drunk at Trinity Well on the borders of the parishes of Bettws Cedewain and Tregynon, Montgomeryshire.

'The people afterwards retire to a green spot for dancing, etc. An old Welsh calendar said that on the eve of Trinity Sunday it is customary to wash or bathe to prevent the tertian ague.'
Revd John Foster, *The Welsh Calendar*, 1895

It is well to employ parsley for the relief of the tertian ague, the juice being taken three days successively, without any other drink. It will stimulate the spirits greatly and strengthen the stomach.

St Oswald, King of Northumbria, in whose vision St Columba of Iona gave him victory over the forces of Cadwallon at Hexham, Northumberland in 634, was killed at Oswestry on 5 August 642

'That night, when Oswald was besieged by the Mercian forces, at the Field of Heaven, he set up the cross of Christ and told his troops to cry out loud: let us pray to the one true God, that he may deliver us from this wicked British king and his commander, for our cause is right. And he dreamed that St Columba stretched his cloak over the sleeping troops, till at dawn they marched out to victory.'

Geoffrey of Monmouth, *History of the Kings of Britain, c.* 1136

According to the Annals of Tigernach, Cú Chullain was born in August in 11 BC

'"A chariot-warrior is driving towards you!" cried the watchman in Emain Macha. "He will shed the blood of every man in the fort unless naked women go out to meet him."

"Send forth naked women to meet him," ordered Conchobor. Then the womenfolk of Emain came forth to meet him and they bared their breasts.

"These are the warriors who will encounter you today."

He hid his face. Then the warriors of Emain seized him and cast him into a tub of cold water. That tub burst about him. The second tub into which he was plunged boiled hands high therefrom. The third tub into which he went after that he warmed so that its heat and cold were properly adjusted for him.

"... One who did that in his seventh year," said Fiachu mac Fir Febe, "it were no wonder that he should triumph over odds ... now that his seventeen years are complete."'

Tain Bo Cuailnge, Recension I, edited and translated by Cecile O'Rahilly

Old Crom Dubh or Garland Sunday is celebrated at Mount Callan in County Clare and at Downpatrick in County Mayo

The ancient Irish idol Crom Dubh (the words mean Stooped and Black) lived just before Saint Patrick came to Ireland. He had two wicked dogs and two wicked sons, and terrorized the countryside.

'. . . the fame of Crom Dubh and his two sons and his two mastiffs, went far and wide, for their evil-doing; and people were so terrified at his name, not to speak of himself, that they used to hide their faces in their bosoms when they used to hear it mentioned in their ears . . . they say that he was a native from hell in the skin of a biped . . . and was the second man that midges ate.'

Douglas Hyde, *Legends of Saints and Sinners*, c. 1900

Court the goddess the weekend after Lammas

'Aine is the queen of the fairies, the moon, mother of the gods, and represented as benign – indeed, the patroness of literature. Bloody sacrifices were made to her. She is on the hills at midsummer, and at the winter feasts, when the spirits of the dead are propitiated. Her influence is particularly powerful on the Friday, Saturday and Sunday following Lammas Day. Her seat at Dunany (Dún Aine, County Louth) is said to have a powerful allure for lunatics, and the sane who sat upon it were risking their sanity.

Fairy-, herb- and charm-mongers believed that Aine possessed unlimited influence over the human frame, regarding her as the "vital spark" which traversed the entire body once every twenty-four hours. Blood-letters would decline to work on a day devoted to Aine, for fear of letting out the vital spark.'

W. G. Wood-Martin, *Traces of the Elder Faiths of Ireland*, 1902

August

Porcine legends

'To be a swine-herd was originally to be a priest in the service of the Death-goddess whose sacred beast was a pig.'

Robert Graves, *The White Goddess*, 1948

Orcus is the Otherworld, or the god of the Otherworld, in Latin (cognate of Greek *erkos*). The Orkneys were known as the Orcades, Islands of the Dead, by the end of the fourth century BC, according to the navigator Pytheas, who got as far as Thule in the Shetland Islands. '*Orc*' means young pig in archaic Gaelic (also a hound, a beagle, a salmon, a whale or an egg).

'When the Fir Volgans [Bolgs] reigned in Ireland, the land was overrun with pigs, which committed vast depredations. The Tuatha de Dananns on conquering the country extirpated all these animals, except one furious herd which devastated the maritime districts of the county of Clare by day, and retired to an island in Malbay, called Muc Inis, now Mutton Island.'

William Hackett, *Porcine Legends*, Kilkenny Archaeological Society, 1852–3

Puck Fair, at Killorglin, County Kerry, is held for three days from 10 August

The first day is called 'gathering day', the second 'fair day', and the third 'scattering day'. The fair is a livestock sale, presided over by a wild goat, brought down from the mountains to stand, garlanded with ribbons, on a platform erected high above the market.

Poc is Irish for billy-goat: the Pooka, which may be met with at Samhain, however, is a vicious and terrifying apparition – a cross between a mule, a bullock and a big black pig.

The end of the Dog Days

The Dog Days, when the Dog Star rises and sets with the Sun, run from 3 July to 11 August and commemorate the period when Sodom and Gomorrah burned.

'It was because of their sins, and more particularly the wicked and detestable vice of homosexuality, that the Welsh were punished by God and so lost first Troy then Britain.'

Gerald of Wales, *Description of Wales*, late twelfth century

'Damn nervous energy and damn efficiency. They have killed good manners as they have killed conversation, for sake of which good manners exist, and they have killed art and literature.'

John Butler Yeats to his son W. B., 11 August 1908

On Old Lammas Day think of the wealth of the world

God the Father: 'Adam behold the fishes
Birds in air and beast
Likewise in land and sea.
Give to them their names
They will come to your command
But do not abash them in any way.'

Adam: 'I name thee Cow, and Bull:
All the cattle separately
Their names let them take

Horse and Mare and Ass,
Dog and Cat and Mouse
Divers Birds and Serpents.

I give names to the Fishes,
Breams, Gurnets and Eels,
I will reckon them all distinctly.'

Gwreans an Bys, 'The Creation of the World: a Cornish Mystery', Bodleian MS N 219, dated 12 August 1611

Collect summer fern beetles for use in amateur dentistry

'Take some lizards, and some of those nasty beetles which are found in ferns in summer time, and burn them to powder in an iron pot. Wet the forefinger of the right hand with the powder, and apply it to the tooth frequently, refraining from licking or spitting it off. Then the tooth will fall away without pain. It is proven.'

Meddygon Myddfai, Welsh, thirteenth century

'In 1861 some tin miners dug up a huge coffin in the defunct church of St James, Tregoney, Cornwall, containing the skeleton of a Cornish giant, who owned a tooth measuring two and a half inches.'

S. P. B. Mais, *The Cornish Riviera*, 1934

'To avoid toothache never shave on a Sunday.'

Lady Wilde, *Medical Superstitions and Ancient Charms*, 1888

Macbeth slew Duncan on this day in 1040: as King of Scotland, he himself was slain by Malcolm Canmore, son of Duncan, on 15 August 1057

'He seems to have represented the Celtic and northern element in the population as against Duncan and his family, who were gradually drawing south and connecting themselves by intermarriage and customs with the Saxons of England and Lothian.'

Dictionary of National Biography, 1893

'On the evening of the 14th August, 1822, his majesty King George IV visiting Scotland, Sir Walter Scott went out in a boat to welcome him and present him with an elegant jewelled cross of St Andrew. When the king was informed of Sir Walter's approach, he exclaimed, "What! Sir Walter Scott? The man in Scotland I most wish to see! Let him come up."'

Chambers and Thomson, *Eminent Scotsmen*, 1870

Lá Féill Móire, festival of Our Lady of the Harvest: the Assumption of the Blessed Virgin

'Early in the morning the people go to the fields and pluck ears of corn, generally bere. These are laid to dry on a rock. When dry they are husked in the hand, winnowed in a fan, ground in a quern, kneaded on a sheep-skin, and formed into a bannock which is called *Moilean Móire*, the fatling of Mary. Bannock toasted before a fire of faggots of rowan, or some other sacred wood and eaten by the family walking sunwise round the fire, singing the Paean of Mary who promised to shield them and did and will shield them from scath till the death of death.

After going round the fire the man puts the embers of the faggot fire with bits of old iron, into a pot which he carries sunwise round the outside of the house and sometimes around the fields and flocks.'

Alexander Carmichael, *Carmina Gadelica*, 1900

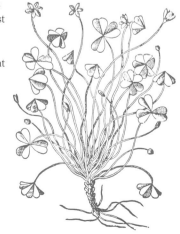

The wonders of Killarney described

'It was August, and the men before Turk Cottage were cutting a second crop of clover, as fine, seemingly, as a first crop elsewhere.'

'Evergreens and other trees, in their brightest livery; blue sky; roaring water, here black, and yonder foaming of a dazzling white; rocks shining in the dark places, or frowning blacks against the light, all the leaves and branches keeping up a perpetual waving and dancing round the cascade: what is the use of putting down all this? A man might describe the cataract of the Serpentine in exactly the same terms, and the reader be no wiser.'

William Thackeray, *The Irish Sketch Book*, 1887

'The Breton peasant fancies that clover sown when the tide is coming in will grow well, but that if the plant be sown at low water or when the tide is going out, it will never reach maturity, and that the cows which feed on it will burst.'

Sir James Frazer, *The Golden Bough*, 1890–1915

ollect Lady's bedstraw, generally still in flower

Our Lady's bedstraw (*Galium verum*) takes its name from the legends that the Virgin Mary gave birth to Christ on a bed of this herb, which as a reward was turned from white to gold. Called *lus-y-volley*, 'sweet-smelling herb', in Manx, this fragrant plant repels evil spirits as well as fleas from the beds of women in childbirth. Also known as a vegetable substitute for rennet in cheesemaking, a producer of red dye, and a prescription against sweaty feet.

The great lexicographer was given *A Description of the Western Islands of Scotland* to read as a boy

In 1773 Dr Samuel Johnson began his long-talked-of tour of the Hebrides, accompanied by his friend and biographer, James Boswell, who later wrote: 'His stay in Scotland was from the 18th August, on which day he arrived, till the 22nd November. I believe ninety-four days were never passed by any man in a more vigorous exertion.'

James Boswell, *Life of Johnson*, 1791

'There is no place so well stored with such great quantities of good beef and mutton where so little of both is consumed by eating. They generally use no fine sauce to entice a false appetite, nor brandy or tea for digestion, the purest water serves them in such cases.'

Martin Martin, *A Description of the Western Islands of Scotland*, 1703

Harvest the 'Good Man's Croft'

'According to Arnot's Edinburgh, the elders of the Scottish church in 1594 exerted their utmost influence to abolish an irrational custom among the husbandmen. The farmers were apt to leave a portion of their land untilled and uncropped year after year; and this spot, which was supposed to be dedicated to Satan, was styled "the Good Man's Croft", that is to say, the landlord's acre. Some pagan ceremony probably had given rise to so strange a superstition; which it is easy to see was designed as a charm or peace offering in behalf of the fertility of the rest of the land.'

John Brand, *Observations on Popular Antiquities*, 1900

The holiday season: things look different away from home

'Four men of the isle of Skye and Harries having gone to Barbadoes, stayed there for fourteen years; and though they were wont to see the Second Sight in their native country, they never saw it in Barbadoes.'

Revd M. Fraser, *A Treatise on the Second Sight*, 1819

'Being in Tipperary, I took the opportunity to visit the famous Rock of Cashel. The cathedral was set on fire in 1495 by the Earl of Kildare, who made the well-known apology to the King, that he would not have done it if he had known that the Archbishop was not inside.'

Letter from Ireland in *The Times*, 20 August 1886

August

A good birthday for engineers and inventors

Thomas Telford was born in 1757, the son of a Dumfriesshire shepherd. His road from London to Holyhead includes the remarkable 570-foot-span Menai Suspension Bridge (built 1819–26). 'The first three-masted vessel passed under the bridge in 1826. Her topmasts were nearly as high as a frigate, but they cleared twelve feet and a half below the centre of the roadway.'

In 1754 William Murdock was born near Auchinleck. He was sent by James Watt to Cornwall to make the mining engines. In 1784 he constructed the model of a high-pressure engine to run on wheels at Redruth, and invented a great many other labour-saving devices. He began to distil coal gas at Redruth in 1792, when he illumined his own home with it.

Chambers and Thomson, *Eminent Scotsmen*, 1870

The hoard from Llyn-Cerrig-Bach, Anglesey, was recovered in August 1943

Once part of a lost lake, the site contained weapons, chariot parts, tools, trumpets and cauldrons, thought to be votive offerings made between *c.* 150 BC and AD 150.

In AD 61 the Roman general Suetonius Paulinus crossed the Menai Strait with a great force and destroyed a Druid centre: 'The Druids were ranged in order, with hands uplifted, invoking the gods, and pouring forth horrible imprecations. The novelty of the sight struck the Romans with awe and terror . . . [but] they felt the disgrace of yielding to a troop of women and a band of fanatic priests. The island fell . . . the religious groves, dedicated to superstition and barbarous rites, were levelled.'

Tacitus, *Annals*, XIV, translated by A. Murphy

'None knoweth, save God and the world's divines and Druids assiduous, how many were of us, that golden torqued host, at the river of Rhiweirth.'

Cynddelw Bryddydd Mawr, twelfth century

Eve of the feast of *sen Padraig*, Patricius senex, or the 'senior Patrick'

Opinions differ, but it may well be that the earlier of the two fifth-century missionaries to Ireland called St Patrick was actually a John the Baptist figure to his later namesake. He was Palladius, sent by Pope Celestine in AD 431, according to the Annals of Inisfallen and the Annals of Ulster, and known as Patricius in Ireland. He died in 461 and is associated with Glastonbury, Somerset, where he may have been buried. His successor, the Saint Patrick whose feast day is on 17 March, arrived to preach in Ireland *c*. 461 and died *c*. 492.

T. F. O'Rahilly, *The Two Patricks*, 1942

Today is also the eve of the feast day of Saint Bartholomew, and the time by which grain crops should be secured and threshing flails prepared.

Virgo

In Virgo they who shall be born are likely to live; he who takes to his bed is quickly healed and his navel and stomach suffer most; he who takes to flight you shall not discover; he who is in chains shall not be loosed.

Apostle: James
Ruler: Neptune

Medieval Irish Zodiac, Basle Library

Stomach ache, a desperate remedy

'When a patient is in desperation put a rope around his feet and hang him by the heels from the rafters. Repeat at reasonable intervals: "This will undo the knot in the guts." '

Old Cures from South Uist

'If you desire to die, eat cabbage in August.'

Book of Iago ab Dewi, Welsh, fourteenth century

August

At sea, observe the customs of the fishermen

In 1894 two fishermen of Aberdeen insisted that a sudden squall was caused by the mention of a hare in the boat.

'It was not permitted when fishing to mention anything *rua* (brown or red-haired). When I used to go fishing I remember when Peaidí Rua – a man who lived in Ventry parish – was mentioned that he was not called Paddy the Red but Peaidí Deaghdhathach (the good-coloured).'

Article in *Béaloideas*, 1927

Neither should the fisher allow talk of a priest, pig or weasel; fish with two others of the same name as himself; bail water out of the boat on the way to the fishing grounds; or ever smoke while at work.

A malediction against fishermen

'May there be a fox on your fishing-hook and a hare on your bait, and may you kill no fish until St Brigid's Day!'

Seán O'Súilleabháin, *Irish Folk Custom and Belief*, 1967

Gerald of Wales

'He was born in August. He sees an inch before his nose.'

Fergusson, *Scottish Proverbs*, 1641

Gerald of Wales was born about 1146: at the time of his election as Bishop of St David's in the summer of 1176 it was said that he was just completing his twentieth year at the time of the birth of Philip Augustus in August 1165.

'Proud of his knowledge of Welsh, though at the same time far from proficient in the tongue, he was always willing to try his hand at the interpretation of Welsh place-names, a pursuit as fascinating for him as for others in our own day no less slenderly equipped than he was.'

Sir John Edward Lloyd, *A History of Wales*, 1911

'Did you treat your Mary Anne to dulse and yellowman
At the Ould Lammas Fair at Ballycastle, O?'

'The marriageable girls of Rathlin Island would always take a sweating-bath to improve their complexions before the annual visit to this fair on the last Tuesday in the month.'

E. Estyn Evans, *Irish Folk Ways*, 1957

Yellowman is a toffee, hammered from a large block, made of butter, brown sugar, golden or corn syrup, baking soda and vinegar.

Irish *duilesc*, called dulse (Latin, *Palmaria palmata*), and laver (*Porphyra umbilicalis*) are seaweeds which are preserved by drying and used, especially in Ireland and Wales, as vegetables, as seasoning in soups, and in the making of a nutritious loaf. According to the Hymn of Columba the monks of the early church gathered dulse and other seaweeds for their food.

'Dulse, fresh from the shore and eaten raw is a South Uist remedy for indigestion.'

Old Cures from South Uist

The Drutheen Charm, to find a
lover's initial

'Slow crawl'd the snail, and if I right can spell,
In the soft ashes marked a curious L;
Oh, may the wondrous omen prove!
For L is found in Lubberkin and Love.'

Sir William Wilde, *Irish Popular Superstitions*, 1852

When in Western Cork on a damp summer's day, look out for the Kerry slug. Unlike most slugs, he is black with white spots, and is only found in Northern Spain, Western France and South-West Ireland.

Decollation of St John the Baptist: *gwyl Ieuan y Moch*, St John's feast of the pig. In the Welsh Laws pannage began in the woods today

'The Flurry Knoxes were, for the moment, in residence at Aussolas, while old Mrs Knox made her annual pilgrimage to Buxton. They were sent there to keep the servants from fighting, and because John Kane had said there was no such enemies to pigs as servants on board-wages. (A dark saying, bearing indirectly on the plenishing of pig-buckets.)'

Somerville and Ross, 'Sharper than a ferret's tooth', *Some Experiences of an Irish R. M.*, 1899

'A quiet pig eats most.'

Hebridean proverb

On this day in 1930 the thirty-six people of St Kilda left their island, no longer able to support themselves without help from the mainland.

In August the turves cut in April or May are brought down from the mountain bog: a week of cutting makes enough fuel for one family

1716: 'Talking about Ireland he (Dr Tilly) told me that there are no vipers nor snakes nor moles there, but he has seen a great many spiders . . . He told me also that the coal which they burn there never flames nor smokes but burns exceeding clear and strong like a red-hot iron. Blowing it will put it out and so will stirring it. The coal is large and very hard and requires an hour at least to light it.'

Dudley Ryder, *Diary*, 1715–16

To procure an easy delivery

'In the end of August, 1836, wrote the author of a "New History of Aberdeenshire",
the writer witnessed the chairing of twelve full-bodied women, who had that
morning come from Speyside, over twenty miles, to undergo the operation. This is
Cloch na Bhan (Stone of the Women), a huge granite rock on top of Meall-ghaineah,
a hill on the east side of Glen Avon, near the boundary between Braemar and
Kirkmichael.'

J. M. McPherson, *Primitive Beliefs in the North-East of Scotland*, 1929

No siestas are allowed in August, and no marriages – as the children are *mic'hiek*
[French, *morveux*; English, snot-nosed or 'mardy'].

Breton

SEPTEMBER

mid-autumn

Breton: *Gwengolo*   Cornish: *Gwengala*
Irish: *Mean Fhómhair*   Manx: *Mean Fouyir*
Scottish: *Meitheamh an Foghmair*   Welsh: *Medi*

A Manx mine

'Written within the mouth of the Brada
Mine, 1st Septr, 1855, from whence I
went down on the shore of the little bay
below the mouth of the mine, looking
nearly south; the dreadful rock with its
chasm at its brow above me; the rock
with a slit like a narrow window on my
left; huge rocks that seem to have
tumbled from the brow of Brada on my
right lying in the sea, and forming a
west fence to the bay, waves roaring and spraying.

   When inside the mine shouted but could make nobody hear; indeed I afterwards
learned that there was nobody at work there that day, the miners having received
their wages the night before and being all drinking about; returned in triumph,
bearing a piece from the top of the mine; saw Peyrick Hodyell on my way back,
whom I told how I had got on; went to Clugston's; boy bitten by dog; said I should
stay another night; afterwards walked to Port Mary.'

George Borrow's diary, 'Expedition to the Isle of Man', 1855

The Galway oyster festival is held each year at the beginning of September

In Cornwall 'oysters are extremely plentiful . . . Mr Carew . . . tells us of
one whose shell being opened as usual at the time of the flood, three
mice eagerly attempted to seize it; but the oyster clasping fast its
shell, killed them all.'

J. Britton and E. W. Brayley, *The Beauties of England and Wales*, 1802

Oysters are good both raw and cooked: swirl them
around a pan in hot butter and eat them on toast, or
sprinkle them with breadcrumbs and a little butter and
grill them, putting a squeeze of lemon on the result.

September

Highland remedies

'Fluxes were cured by the use of meadow sweet, or jelly of bilberry, or a poultice of flour and suet; or newly churned butter; or strong creme and fresh suet boiled, and drank plentifully morning and evening.'

Thomas Pennant, *A Tour in Scotland and Voyage to the Hebrides*, 1772

A sailor's cure for the morning after

(from the late master of the motor vessel *Lochmor*).

'Take a bunch of sea pinks pulled with the roots. Boil for an hour or more. Leave to cool. Drink slowly and you are ready for the next night ashore.'

Old Cures from South Uist

The worship and sacrifice of animals continued in Celtic lands until quite recent times

This is manifest by the fierce denunciation of certain practices. The Presbytery of Dingwall, Ross, on 5 September 1656, made special reference to the heathenish customs, then prevalent in the North, of pouring out libations of milk upon the hills, of adoring stones and wells, and, above all, of sacrificing bulls.

In 1678 four men were tried 'for sacrificing a bull in a heathenish manner in the Island of St Ruffus, for the recovery of health of Cirstane Mackenzie'.

James Bonwick, *Irish Druids and Old Irish Religions*, 1894

'It was commonly said in Ireland that bull's blood was used in mixing the mortar for castles. There certainly seem to have been animal sacrifices under the sites of buildings, either to assuage the feelings of the displaced spirit of the site, or to provide a guardian spirit for the house. One explanation, however, for the burial of horse skulls found under floors and in walls is that they gave the room a resonant sound for dancing.'

Seán O'Súilleabháin, *Nósanna agus Piseoga na nGael*, 1967

5 In early September 1715, James, called the Old Pretender, was proclaimed king by the disaffected populace of St Columb in Cornwall

A predecessor of his, James IV of Scotland, who died at the battle of Flodden Field, may have been the author of this expression of innocent delight:

'Quhen Tayis bank was blumit bricht
With blossomis bricht and braid,
Be that river ran I doun richt
Undir the ryss, I reid.
The merle melit with hir micht,
And mirth in morning maid;
Throw solace, sound, and semelie sicht
Also ane sang I said.'

6 Watch out for unusual beasts

'There are in Skye neither rats or mice, but the weasel is so frequent, that he is heard in houses rattling behind chests or beds, as rats in England.'
Dr Johnson, September 1773

'Dr Matheson was at the time enjoying a sail on Loch Alsh, which separates the Island of Skye from the mainland. We were going gaily along, when suddenly I saw something rise out of the Loch in front of us – a long, straight, neck-like thing as tall as my mast. It was not a sea-serpent, but a much larger and more substantial beast – something in the nature of a giant lizard, I should think.'
The Strand Magazine, September 1893

September

The Reaping Race

'As the day advanced people gathered from all quarters watching the reapers. The sun rose into the heaven. There was a fierce heat. Not a breath of wind. The rye-stalks no longer moved. They stood in perfect silence, their heads a whitish colour, their stalks golden. Already there was a large irregular gash in the rye, ever increasing. The bare patch, green with little clover plants that had been sown with rye, was dotted with sheaves, already whitening in the hot sun.Through the hum of conversation the regular crunching of the reaping-hooks could be heard.'

Liam O'Flaherty, 1937, who died this day in 1984

'In Upper Brittany the last sheaf is always made into human shape; but if the farmer is a married man, it is made double and consists of a little corn-puppet placed inside a large one. This is called the Mother-sheaf. It is delivered to the farmer's wife who unties it and gives drink-money in return.'

The Gentleman's Magazine, 1795

Gwyl Fair y Medi: St Mary's Feast in reaping time

Swallows traditionally leave Wales.

Swallows are well-regarded on Irish farms and farmers dislike any interference with their nests. It is believed in Wicklow that if a swallow flies into the house good luck will ensue, but if a bird is killed the cows will milk blood.

'The bird swerved dapple-white in the blue sky, paused, and then swam into the commotion of rays between the sun and the lake.
The sleek wings vibrating in the still air stirred a venture in the heart, and yielding to the brightness, every fear fled with the wonder of the flight.'

Euros Bowen (b. 1904), *Winged in Gold*

To the Earl of Argyll before the Battle of Flodden, fought this day in 1513

'It is fitting to rise up against the English, we expect no hesitant uprising; the edges of swords, the points of spears, it is right to ply them gladly.

Let us make harsh and mighty warfare against the English, I tell you, before they have taken our native land; let us not give up our country, but anxiously watch over our patrimony just like the Gael of Ireland.'

Scottish/Irish, author unknown, 1513

'And then followed the most fearful and tragic part of the battle, for the remnant of the Scots, who still struggled round their King, threw themselves into a circle, and fought with the courage of heroes, – that awful struggle of giants.'
'The resting place of the monarch has never been clearly ascertained. Tradition says that the skeleton of a man, encircled by an iron chain (said to have been the body of James from the fact of his always wearing one as a penance for aiding in the death of his father), was found in a cell in the fortress of Lord Home.'

Edmund Bogg, *A Thousand Miles of Wandering in the Border Country*, 1898

Brittany, September 1812

'Between the sea and the land lies a pelagic country, the boundaries between the two elements uncertain: the skylark flies with the lark of the sea, the shore lark; the plough and the boat are a stone's throw from each other, both land and water are furrowed. The seafarer and the herdsman borrow each other's language: the sailor speaks of fleecy clouds – the shepherd talks of flotillas of sheep. The sands of many shades, banks of many kinds of shellfish, the seaweed, the fringes of silver foam etching the green or flaxen borders of the wheatfields. I do not know in what isle of the Mediterranean I have seen a better bas-relief of the Nereids fastening festoons to the hem of the robe of Ceres.'

Chateaubriand, *Mémoires d'outre-tombe*, 1849

September

Fiddlers are busy all year round

11

'Sunday night would be the principal night for the dance, not Saturday night. Saturday was the night when you left everything ready for the next day. If it was the time of year when you dug the potatoes as you used them, you dug as much on Saturday as done you Sunday, and several other things like that. Anyway, everyone had to get up on Sunday morning to go to church, so you couldn't be too late on Saturday night.

But Sunday night there were dances everywhere, because no-one gave a hoot about the rest of the week.'

Packie Manus Byrne, *Recollections of a Donegal Man*, edited by Stephen Jones, 1989

12

**'I was born in Belfast between the mountain and the gantries
To the hooting of lost sirens and the clang of trams.'**

(Frederick) Louis MacNeice was born on 12 September 1907, and died of viral pneumonia on 3 September 1963 after recording underground in Yorkshire.

'It's no go my honey love, it's no go my poppet;
Work your hands from day to day, the winds will blow the profit.
The glass is falling hour by hour, the glass will fall for ever,
But if you break the bloody glass you won't hold up the weather.'

From 'Bagpipe Music'

'The little bird which has whistled from the end of a bright-yellow bill: it utters a note above Belfast Loch – a blackbird from a yellow-heaped branch.'

Anon, Irish, ninth century, translated by Gerard Murphy

By the end of the summer the sorrel has turned red: pluck the whole plant to fix indigo blue

'Save household urine until there is sufficient in a big tub beside the fire. Keep the tub at a steady 85–90 degrees. Put the indigo in a little bag of muslin and steep it in the urine. Every three days squeeze it well to take the colour out.

About an ounce of indigo to a pound of wool, but the strength varies. Take sorrel, root and stem, wash it but do not break it. Boil this plant, a pound to a pint, until the juice is strong. Strain it and add to the urine. This is the mordant and makes the colour adhere to the wool. Remove the indigo bag when this is done.

Wash the wool in clean hot water and put in the urine tub. Cover the tub and leave for three days, squeezing the fabric every day. Remember that the temperature must always be the same.

After three days put back the "blue" bag and make and add the sorrel juice as before. Repeat every three days until the colour is right. For medium blue it may take a week, for dark blue a month. When the colour is as you want it wash the wool in soft water and with a soap that will not make the fibres brittle. In Uist the water in the streams is particularly soft from peat, or else use rain water. Dry in the open on heather or the clean grass.'

Peigi MacRae, North Glendale
Recipes for the Dyeing of Wool

Holy Cross Day: sudden showers are frequent

'Give me more love, or more disdaine:
The Torrid, or the frozen Zone,
Bring equall ease unto my paine;
The temperate affords me none.
Either extreme, of love, or hate,
Is sweeter than a calm estate.

Give me a storme; if it be love,
Like *Danae* in that golden showre
I swimme in pleasure; if it prove
Disdain, that torrent will devoure
My Vulture-hopes; and he's possest
Of Heaven, that's but from Hell release:
Then crowne my joyes, or cure my paine;
Give me more love, or more disdaine.'

'Mediocritie in love rejected', Thomas Carew (1594/5–1640), Cornishman

September

As the dusk falls earlier it may be useful to be able to identify a fairy

'Their Apparell and Speech is like that of the people and Countrey under which they live; so are they seen to wear Plaids and variegated Garments in the Highlands of Scotland, and Suanochs therefore in Ireland. They speak but little, and that by way of whistling, clear, not rough.'

Revd Robert Kirk, Minister at Aberfoyle, *The Secret Commonwealth*, 1691

'Specimens of this Danann race still exist, but have gradually mixed with their forerunners to the present day. Every one who is fair-haired, vengeful, large, and every plunderer, professors of musical and entertaining performances, who are adepts of Druidical and magical arts, they are the descendants of the Tuatha-de-Dananns.'

Dubhaltach MacFirbisigh, *Chronicum Scotorum: A Chronicle of Irish Affairs from the Earliest Times to 1135*, seventeenth century

Feast day of Saint Cornelius

'The people have a singular custom whenever their cattle are diseased amongst these stones (at Carnac), to pray to St Cornelius for recovery. Such a practice may be a remnant of Pagan superstition.'

Mrs Charles Stothard, *Letters Written during a Tour . . . in 1818*

A Montgomeryshire practice of healing *foul* or foot-rot in a cow was to watch her closely if she lay down, and to throw the piece of turf where her bad foot had been placed into a thorn bush.

Today is also the feast day of Saint Cyprian

'At the festival of Ciaran son of the carpenter wild geese come over the cold sea; at the festival of Cyprian, a mighty counsel, the red stag bells from the brown plain.'

Durham Cathedral Library, Hunter MS 100

17

A good day to consider your health

'In September take three draughts of milk in the morning daily. After this you may take what you wish, for vegetables and fruit are now ripe, though bread is apt to be mouldy. Whosoever is bled on the 17th day of September, will not be attacked by colic, ague nor cough that year.'

Meddygon Myddfai, Welsh, thirteenth century

Gather the leaves of oak trees in August or September

'Dry them well and keep covered. If applied to any contused integument, or watery excoriation, they will heal it. Ripe acorns, too, crisply roast and kept in a covered oaken vessel, freshly ground and mixed with milk, or with wheaten flour to make bread, is good for weak persons, those subject to affections of the lungs.'

Meddygon Myddfai, Welsh, thirteenth century

18

Domestic bliss for the ladies of Plas Newydd, Llangollen

They eloped from Kilkenny in 1775 and lived in Welsh harmony for fifty years, making a Gothic house and beautiful garden, dressed in men's clothes.

'Rose at seven. soft morning inclined to rain. went the rounds after Breakfast. Our shoes from Chirk. vile. scolded Thomas for growing fat. from ten to one writing and reading (La Rivalité) to my beloved. She drawing. spent half an hour in the shrubery. mild grey day. from half past one till three reading. from four till seven read to my Sally finished La Rivalité began Warton on Milton. in the Shrubery till eight. Powell returned from Wrexham. no letters. eight till nine read l'Esprit des croisades. papered our Hair. an uninterrupted delightful day.'

Lady Eleanor Butler's diary, 18 September 1785

As Quarter Day approaches attend to financial matters

'I neither praise poverty, nor at it repine
But who praises me poverty, I would let him have mine
The poor man despised without money or food or wine
He is in the light always, despite how the sun may shine.'
Douglas Hyde, 'A Few Rhymed Proverbs', *Celtic Review*, 1904–5

'Rannaidh bocht a' beagán' – 'the poor will share their little amount.'
Donegal proverb

'Oh Thady Brady you are my darlin'
You are my looking-glass from night till morning,
I love you better without one farthin'
Than Brian Gallagher with house and garden.'
Irish ballad

Harvest Cripple Goat

'In this Hyperborean country (the Isle of Skye) in
every district, there is to be met with a rude
stone consecrated to Gruagach or Apollo.
The first who is done with his reaping
send a man or a maiden with a bundle of
Corn to his next neighbour, who has not
yet reaped down his Harvest, who when he
has finished, dispatches to his own next
neighbour, who is behind in his work,
and so on, until the whole corns are cut
down. This sheaf is called the Cripple Goat, or Gaobhir
Bhacagh, and is at present meant as a brag or affront to the farmer, for being more
remiss, or later than the others at reaping the harvest, for which reason the bearer
of it must make as good a pair of heels, for fear of being ill-used for his indiscretion,
as he can. Whether the appellation of Cripple Goat may have any or the least
adherence to the Apollonian Altar of Goats Horns, I shall not pretend to determine.'
Sir James Frazer, *The Golden Bough*, 1890–1915

Loss of the Manx herring fleet on St Matthew's Day, 1787

'On Thursday 20th September, 1787, an unusually large quantity of fish was brought into Douglas, and the weather was beautifully fine. In the evening of that day, being St Matthew's Eve, the whole fleet numbering, it is said, 400 boats, proceeded to the fishing ground (at that time of the year the herring have moved from the western coast of the island, off Peel to the eastern coast, off Clay-head and Laxey, about three leagues from Douglas). But a brisk equinoctial gale sprang up at midnight, and the fleet headed for the harbour, where most of the pier and the lighthouse at the end of it had been destroyed earlier in the year and a lonely lantern hung in its place. As the weather worsened, the lantern was lost and the fleet were thrown against each other and the remains of the pier. A ballad commemorating the occasion gives the number of dead as twenty-one.'

William Harrison, *Mona Miscellany, c.* 1870

Grace O'Malley of Connaught, pirate

'A woman that hath impudently passed the part of womanhood and been a great spoiler and chief commander and director of thieves and murderers at sea to spoile this province', met Queen Elizabeth I in September 1593 at Greenwich Castle and obtained a pardon.

Tradition has it that her son Theobald (recorded in the State papers as 'Tibbot-na-Long'), was born about the year 1567 on board one of his mother's ships, and that the day after his birth the ship was attacked by Turkish corsairs. The battle was going badly for the Irish, and the captain requested Grace to come on deck to give heart to her men. Grace, furious, emerged on deck firing at the Turks: 'Take this from unconsecrated [i.e. unchurched] hands.'

Calendar of Carew MSS

September

The full moon nearest the autumnal equinox rises at the same time for several days

'How far from the Earth to the Moon? Answer: one *toin* and a half, and the same between the Moon and Mercury from Mercury to Venus one *toin*. The *toin* is five thousand *stadia*: one *stadia* is twenty thousand and five paces. A pace is two steps, and a step two feet. Each foot is eight inches.'

Arundel MS 333, Irish, 1514–19

In Libra he who fleeth by sea shall come into peril; they that shall be born shall encounter peril; they that withdraw themselves shall not be found; he who falls into a danger . . . [?] a lantern

Apostle: Andrew
Ruler: Orcus

Medieval Irish Zodiac, Basle Library

To the victor the *sméar* – the choicest, or blackberry

'The Carl of the Drab Coat came bumping and stumping and clumping into the camp and was surrounded by a multitude that adored him and hailed him with tears.

"Meal!" he bawled, "meal for the love of the stars!"

And he bawled "Meal, meal!" until he bawled everybody into silence.

Fionn addressed him.

"What for, the meal, dear heart?"

"For the inside of my mouth," said the Carl, "for the recesses and crannies and deep-down profundities of my stomach. Meal, meal!" he lamented.

Meal was brought.

The Carl put his coat on the ground, opened it carefully, and revealed a store of blackberries, squashed, crushed, mangled, democratic, ill-looking.

"The meal!" he groaned, "the meal!"

It was given to him.

"What of the race, my pulse?" said Fionn.

"Wait, wait," cried the Carl. "I die, I die for meal and blackberries." '

James Stephens, *Irish Fairy Tales*, 1920, from B.L. Egerton 154, a nineteenth-century MS by Edward O'Reilly

Holy Rood Day, Old Style

The fourth Sunday in September is the Butter Festival Pardon in St-Herbert.

Recipe for Breton Butter Cake

Take half a pound of lightly salted butter, softened, and beat it. In a separate bowl beat 7 oz. of castor sugar, the yolks of 4 medium eggs, 2 fl. oz. of sweet white wine and the seeds of 1 vanilla pod until the mixture turns white. Sift 7 oz. of plain flour and 1 level teaspoon of baking powder and fold them into the mixture, and then whisk in the butter. Whisk the egg whites to stiff peaks and gradually fold in the meringue mixture. Bake at gas mark 5 or 375F in a greased eight-inch tin for thirty minutes.

Butter was buried in the bog, for safe, cool keeping, and kegs dating from prehistoric times are still occasionally dug up.

'Lachlan and Hector, the two brothers who founded the fortunes of the MacLeans, came to John MacDonald, first Lord of the Isles, in quest of their fortunes, and MacKinnon, who was MacDonald's master of the household, was bitterly jealous of them. He set before them bread and "gruthim" – butter and curds mixed together, made in the time of Harvest and kept until Lent. The gruthim was so brittle that the men could not take it up on their long knives, and MacKinnon told them that if they could not eat the meat as it was they should put it on the nebs of hens. For this insult the MacLeans murdered MacKinnon.'

I. F. Grant, *Highland Folk Ways*, 1961

The corvid family

'The Cornish Nightingales, as they call them (the Cornish Cough [chough] a sort of Jackdaw if I mistake not) a little black bird which makes them a visit about Michaelmas.'

Celia Fiennes, *Journal*, late seventeenth century

All members of the corvid family figure in the ancient religious beliefs of the Celtic

lands. King Arthur himself was said to have returned as a chough, though whether he danced in the communal courtship ceremony with his fellow birds is not recorded. Since 1952 the red-billed, red-legged bird has not been seen in Cornwall where it has so many names – Cornish jack, Cornish kae (its cry is a high-pitched *kee-ow*), palores, even market jew crow – and is rare in Ireland, where it is known as the sea crow.

September

The afternoon of the Sunday immediately preceding St Michael's Day is specially devoted by the women and girls to procuring carrots and is known as *Domhnach Curran*

'Three plants which the people call carrots grow in Uist: the *daucus carota*, the original of the cultivated carrot; *daucus maritimus*, a long, slender carrot much like the parsnip in appearance and flavour, and it is rare in the British Isles, and the *conium*, or hemlock, which resembles the carrot and is occasionally mistaken for it. It is hard, acrid and poisonous.'

Alexander Carmichael, *Carmina Gadelica*, 1900

Carrots with cream
Take a pound of young carrots and cook them to taste. Warm 2 oz. butter with a tablespoon of thick cream, add salt and pepper and pour over the carrots, before serving them garnished with plenty of parsley.

Every season has its pleasure

'Pleasant are fruits in the season of autumn
also pleasant is wheat on the stalk;
pleasant is the sun in the cloudless sky,
pleasant is the eagle on the shore of the sea when it is in flood,
also pleasant are seagulls at play;
pleasant is May for the cuckoos and the nightingale,
also pleasant when the weather is better.
Pleasant is the moon shining on the world,
pleasant is the summer and the calm long day;
pleasant are flowers at the top of fragrant bushes,
pleasant are the lonely doe and the hind;
pleasant is the vegetable garden when the leek flourishes,
also pleasant is the charlock in the young plants;
pleasant is the heath when it is heathery,
also pleasant is the sea-marsh for cattle.'

The Pleasant Things of Taliesin, Welsh, sixth century

Michaelmas: Michael is the patron saint of the sea, boats and horses

Temples were dedicated to him round the coasts wherever Celts were situated –
at Mont St Michel in Brittany and at St Michael's Mount in Cornwall, and Aird
Michael in South and in North Uist.

'The Eve of St Michael is for bringing in carrots, baking the struan, killing the
lamb, of stealing the horses.
The Day of St Michael is the day of early mass, the sacrificial lamb; the oblation
struan; the distribution of the lamb; of pilgrimage to the burial ground of their
fathers; the day of giving and receiving carrots with their wishes and
acknowledgements, and the day of athletics and racing horses.
And the Night of Michael is the night of the dance and the song, of merry making
and love making and love-gifts.'

Alexander Carmichael, *Carmina Gadelica*, 1900

'From Michaelmas till the
25th March, during the
cold season of the Year
only, did the close
study last.'

*The Memoirs of the
Marquis of Clanricard,*
1722

**Pilgrimages to Saint Anne d'Auray are made throughout the summer from
7 March to the end of September, chiefly on Wednesdays and Sundays**

Saint Anne, mother of Mary, was said to have been born in Cornouaille, and to have
retired there when her daughter was grown. Jesus often came to visit his
grandmother in Brittany. She is especially petitioned for good harvests.

'Apples, berries, beautiful hazelnuts,
blackberries, acorns from the oak tree,
raspberries, they are the due of generosity,
haws of the prickly sharp hawthorn.'

'Buile Suibhne', Middle Irish MSS

OCTOBER

watery month

Breton: *Here*   Cornish: *Hedra*
Irish: *Deireadh Fhómhair* (end of autumn)   Manx: *Jerrey Fouyir*
Scottish: *Deireadh Fhoghmair*   Welsh: *Hydref*

Recipe for a cobbler

Wholesome fruits of the season include damsons, plums, elderberries and blackberries: wash some and put them together with some sugar and lemon juice into a buttered dish. Cover with pastry and bake in a fairly hot oven for thirty minutes.

'In October drink new wine and eat minnows. Let your diet consist of fresh meat and wholesome vegetables.'

Meddygon Myddfai, Welsh, thirteenth century

Flint arrowheads were popularly thought to be 'Elf shots', and might be used as a charm, but never brought into the house

'As for Elf arrows, the Divell sharpens them with his ain hand, and deliveris them to Elf boys, wha whyttilis and dightis them with a sharp thing lyk a paking needle; bot when I was in Elfland, I saw them whyttling and dighting them.'

Isobel Gowdie, Morayshire witch, 1662, from R. Pitcairn, *Scottish Criminal Trials*

Fairies were often blamed for casting these weapons at grazing cattle in an effort to take them to their own world. A cure was to make the affected animal drink water in which the arrowhead had been boiled.

Use iron to ward off the Little People: iron nails in the cradle will protect the occupant from substitution for a changeling; a smoothing iron under the bed and a sickle in the window is a sensible precaution for all.

Anyone entering a fairy dwelling should take care to strike a knife or other piece of worked metal (steel is better than iron) into the door so that it may not close behind them.

October

Order a set of winter clothes

'According as I'd finish in one house I'd go to another, principally in the winter, and the season from September up to Christmas.'
Michael Gaynor, tailor, of Roscommon, born 1845, recorded 1932.

Article in *Béaloideas*, 1937

'The costume of both sexes is very peculiar both in cut and colour, but varies considerably in different districts. Bright red, violet, and blue are much used, not only by the women, but in the coats and waistcoats of the men.'

T. A. Trollope, *A Summer in Brittany*, 1840

'The little man pulled out four of his red hairs and blew upon them, and each became a tailor. The first one had a cabbage, the second one a pair of shears, the third had a needle and the fourth an iron. They sat down and went to work. From the first leaf of the cabbage they made a handsome coat; from another a waistcoat, but for the wide trousers of Leon they used two cabbage leaves.'

E. Souvestre, 'The Groac'h from the Isle of Lok', *Le foyer Breton*, 1845

Sea swallows, or common terns, (Latin, *Sterna hirundo*; Irish, *greabhróg*), graceful but aggressive, leave their rocky summer roosts and gather in Dublin Bay before winging southward for the winter

'Saint Cainneach once lived on the Isle of Birds (Inis nÉn) where the birds were very loquacious, and annoyed the Saint who was trying to pray. He rebuked them, therefore, and the birds sat very still until Monday morning.'

Plummer, *Vitae Sanctorum Hiberniae*, 1910

rian O'Nolan, Flann O'Brien and Myles na gCopaleen were born on this day in Strabane, Co. Tyrone in 1911

O'Nolan graduated in Celtic languages from University College, Dublin in 1932 and published novels including *At-Swim-Two-Birds* and *An Béal Bocht* (*The Poor Mouth*) as Flann O'Brien.

He also wrote a column, feted for its unusual humour, in the *Irish Times* under the name Myles na gCopaleen from *c.* 1939 until his death in Dublin on 1 April 1966.

'A lady lecturing recently on the Irish language drew attention to the fact (I mentioned it myself as long ago as 1925) that, while the average English speaker gets along with a mere 400 words, the Irish-speaking peasant uses 4,000. Considering what most English speakers can achieve with their tiny fund of noises, it is a nice speculation to what extremity one would be reduced if one were locked up for a day with an Irish-speaking bore and bereft of all means of committing murder or suicide.'

An Cruiskeen Lawn

'Examination, 5 October 1600, by Sir Harry Vivian of Trelowarren of William Jehoseph, who lately landed at Mounts Bay on return from the English seminary of Valladolid in Spain The examinee spoke of Cornish scholars there. Indeed Philip III and Queen Margaret, on a state visit to the college on the 19th July, 1600 had listened to sermons preached in Cornish and Welsh, as well as in French, Flemish, Italian and English.'

P. Berresford-Ellis, *The Cornish Language and its Literature*, 1974

The October Horse Festival is of Bronze Age origins. The horse is both a magical animal, appearing to the unwary to carry them into the Otherworld, like the kelpie of Highland lore, and a valuable, noble and loyal friend

'Saint Colmcille, knowing that his end was near . . . sat down for a while and rested . . there comes up to him the white horse . . . that used to carry the milk-pail between the cow-pasture and the monastery. The creature putting his head in his bosom; knowing that his master would soon depart from him, began to utter plaintive moans, and as if a man, to shed tears in abundance in the saint's lap.'

St Adamnan, *Life of Columba*, 679–704

'After Edmund Burke's son was killed in the Napoleonic wars, the young man's horse mourned his death on the breast of the great Irish orator himself.'

W. A. O'Conor, *History of the Irish People*, 1886–7

October

Scottish conquest of the Isle of Man

On this day in 1270 the Scots troops disembarked at Derby Haven, and next morning before sunrise a battle was fought, in which 537 islanders fell:

'Ten L's, thrice X, with V and II, did fall;
Ye Manx take care, or suffer more ye shall.'

' "The Manx and Scotch will come so near as to throw their beetles at one another." A traditional prophetic saying used in the north of the island. It is stated in Hollinshed's *Chronicles of Scotland* that Agricola, the Roman general, wanting vessels to carry his army over from Scotland to the Isle of Man, such as could swim and knew the shallow places of the coast made shift to pass the gulf, and so got to land to the great wonder of the inhabitants.

The land is assuredly gaining yearly on the sea, at the Point of Ayre; and the northern look forward to their saying being ultimately fulfilled, notwithstanding there are yet some twenty miles to fill up.'

William Harrison, *Mona Miscellany, c.* 1870

Harvest of the geese

'*Foghmhar na ngéadhna*, harvest of the geese, when the geese are allowed to range the stubble.'

Revd Patrick Dinneen, *Foclóir*, 1927

'They'll give me my pay in a lump when the harvest's done,
I'll tuck it away in a knot in my shirt to keep,
And back to the village, singing and mad for fun –
And I promise I won't spend sixpence until we meet.

For you're a man like myself with an antique thirst,
So need I say how we'll give the story an end?
We'll shout and rattle our cans the livelong night
Till there isn't as much as the price of a pint to spend.'

Eoghan Ruadh Ó'Súilleabháin – 'Owen of the Sweet Mouth' – who died (after a drunken brawl) in 1784. Translated by Frank O'Connor.

Between the two Michaelmasses

'It is an old custom in these parts for the poor people to go about the farm-houses to beg and gather milk between and about the two Michaelmasses, that they may be able to make some puddings and pancakes against Bryngwyn and Clyro Feasts, which are on the same day, next Sunday, the Sunday after Old Michaelmas Day or Hay Fair, October 10th. The old custom is still kept up in Bryngwyn and at some hill farms in Clyro.'

Revd Francis Kilvert, *Diary*, 9 October 1870

Old Michaelmas Day, after which blackberries are wizened and bitter

'The Devil and the birds have spoiled them. I knew an old lady whose birthday always fell on that day and she religiously kept it by eating, for the last time that year, a blackberry tart with clotted cream.'

Miss M. A. Courtney, *Folk-Lore Journal*, 1886

'Yet another day Saint Kieran walked, and in his way there was by chance a brake on which was a great abundance of blackberries; and from his seer's quality he comprehended that these would be needed yet. He provided them with a covering, therefore, that the winter's cold should not touch them, and it was his intent that, though to a year's end they were there, they should be none the worse, if not indeed all the better.'

S. H. O'Grady, *Silva Gadelica*, 1892

October

Feast of Saint Cainneach, Canice; in Scotland, Kenneth

Cainneach, who died in AD 600, was the son of a bard who studied at Glasnevin and Iona and became a friend of Colmcille.

There is a legend that Colmcille was once caught in a storm at sea with some of his monks. Frightened, they begged him to pray for them, but he refused, saying that Cainneach would do the praying, and kept rowing. Cainneach in Aghaboe was about to sit down to a meal when he leapt up and ran to the church, losing a shoe. The storm ceased and Colmcille remarked to his monks that Cainneach's race to the church with one shoe had saved them.

One of his foundations, Cill Chainnigh, has given the name to the modern Irish county, Killkenny.

Columbus Day: Welshman discovered America

Madawg ap Owain Gwynedd was 'a great sailor and the first to discover Tir y Gorllewin, or America. Not many years ago his tomb was discovered there with an inscription in old Welsh – saying who he was, and how he loved the sea. I have seen the lines which were found on the tomb.' His descendants 'are still to be found in a part of America speaking the pure iaith Cymraeg, better Welsh than we of Wales do'.
George Borrow, *Wild Wales*, 1862

' . . . why the Discovery of America was look't on as a Fairie Tale, and the Reporters hooted at as Inventors of ridiculous Utopias, or the first probable Asserters punished as Inventures of new Gods and Worlds.'
Revd Robert Kirk, Minister at Aberfoyle, *The Secret Commonwealth*, 1691

Consider a seventh child: a useful cure for scrofula

'. . . why in England the King cures the Struma by stroaking, and the Seventh Son in Scotland; whither his temperat Complexion conveys a Balsome, and sucks out the corrupting Principles by a frequent warm fanative Contact, or whither the Parents of the Seventh Child put furth a more eminent Virtue to his Production than to all the Rest, as being the certain Meridian and hight to which their Vigour ascends, and from that furth have a graduall declyning into a feebleness of the Bodie and its Production.'

Revd Robert Kirk, Minister at Aberfoyle, *The Secret Commonwealth*, 1691

Neck-lumps, as they were called in Irish (*cnuic bragad*) may be cured by the application of a poultice of 'well-mingled dropping of ancient ganders, and of goats, with lard of aged hens'.

Mining is an ancient and dangerous activity to which the Welsh and Cornish, especially, are accustomed

'People that know very little of arts or sciences or of the powers of Nature will laugh at us Cardiganshire miners that maintain the being of knockers in mines – a kind of good natured impalpable people but to be seen and heard, and who seem to us to work in the mines . . . Three or four miners together shall hear them sometimes, but if the miners stop to take notice of them the knockers will also stop; but let the miners go on at their own work, – suppose it is boring – the knockers will also go on as brisk as can be in landing, blasting, or beating down the loose.'

Lewis Morris (1700–1765), *A Book of Wales*, edited by D. M. and E. M. Lloyd, 1953

October

Do not harm the cat who guards the granary

'Whoever kills the cat that guards the king's barn, or steals it, its head is to be set down on a clean level floor, and its tail is to be held up, and then wheaten grains are to be poured around it until they cover the tip of its tail. Any other cat is worth four legal pence . . . In law, essential qualifications of a cat are that it should be perfect of ear and eye and tail and teeth and claws, not singed by the fire; and that it should kill mice and not eat its kittens, and should not be caterwauling every full moon . . .'

Medieval Welsh Laws

Saint Kildans kept very few pets. But every household had at least one cat to defend the stores from mice.

Oscar Wilde was born this day in 1854

'If one could only teach the English how to talk and the Irish how to listen, society would be quite civilized.'

'The *Leanan-sidhe*, or the spirit of life, was supposed to be the inspirer or the poet and singer, as the *Ban-sidhe* was the spirit of death and foreteller of doom.'

Lady Wilde, *Ancient Legends of Ireland*, 1888

W. B. Yeats, however, believed that the spirit consumed as it inspired, so that the lives of poets and singers are brief.

'The *Lianhan Shee*, your reverence, is never seen, only by thim it keeps wid; but – hem! – it always, wid the help of the ould boy, conthrives, sir, to make the person break the agreement, an' thin it has thim in its power.'

William Carleton (1794–1869), *The Lianhan Shee*

Light the rush lights, the nights are drawing in

Legend has it that St Patrick cursed the rush, which pricked him when he sat down, so that every green blade has a brown tip.

'The rush, common in boglands, was never a despised plant: it was gathered in quantity every year for making lights, strewing on the floor, weaving ropes, mats, baskets, and Saint Bridget's crosses, harvest knots, and Hallowe'en rush ladders.'
E. Estyn Evans, *Irish Folk Ways*, 1957

In Wales the occasion of renewing the rushes on the floor of the church was a day of celebration; the rushes were accompanied by music and dancing.

St Luke's Day

'The festival of Saint Luke, the Evangelist, today is called St Luke's Little Summer in England and *Haf Bach Mihangel* [Michael the archangel], the autumnal summer, in Wales.'
Revd John Fisher, *The Welsh Calendar*, 1895

On this day the congregations of the Welsh borders were, until late in the nineteenth century, accustomed to pelt their preachers with crab-apples.

'Burn not the precious apple tree of spreading and low-sweeping bough: tree ever decked in bloom of white, against whose fair head all men put forth the hand.'
'Death of Fergus', Irish, early sixteenth century, B.L. Egerton MS 1782

On this day in 1745 Jonathan Swift, Dean of St Patrick's Cathedral, Dublin, died, aged 77, having long before composed:

'His Grace!* impossible! what, dead!
Of old age too, and in his bed!
And could that mighty warrior fall?
And so inglorious, after all!
Well, since he's gone, no matter how,
The last loud trump must wake him now;
And trust me, as the noise grows stronger,
He'd wish to sleep a little longer.
And could he be indeed so old
As by the newspapers we're told?
Threescore, I think, is pretty high;
T'was time in conscience he should die.
This world he cumber'd long enough;
He burnt his candle to the snuff.'

*John Churchill, Duke of Marlborough, the Williamite commander who captured Cork and Kinsale in 1691

Jonathan Swift, 'A Satirical Elegy on the Death of a Late Famous General', 1722

A Breton knows the value of a good sponsor for his child

'I want a just man to be godfather to my son.'
'A just man? Well, I think I am a just man.'
'Who are you then?'
'Saint Peter.'
'Well, then you are not a just man.'
'I – not a just man?' Saint Peter replied somewhat nettled. 'Please tell me why, my good man.'
'Why? That I can tell you: because I am told you refuse entry for really minor sins, for nothing at all, for miserable trifles, and this to decent, hardworking people like myself. Why? Because maybe they do drink a mug of cider too many on a Sunday after working hard all week.'

Breton folktale, told by J. Corvez of Plourez-Finistère, 1876

Two customs proper and peculiar to the Irishry

'The one was Fostering; the other Gossipred; both of which have ever bin of greater estimation among this people, then with any other Nation in the Christian world.'

John Davies, *A Discovery of the True Causes why Ireland was never entirely Subdued*, 1612

Life's quietus is reviewed as the days shorten

Bás sona, or 'happy death' is a phrase used by the Catholic communities in the west of Scotland and Ireland. It means that the dying person has been confessed and anointed, and the death-hymn intoned.

'There is one other custome in the highlands, when a gentleman dyes so manie women liveing under himself, especialie of the meaniest sort & though they live elsewher (though perhaps they never sawe him in the face) if they be his relations or if he has done them much kyndnes, heareing his deatht they come to the house and entreing in, they weep and cry very loud called in Irish *Koranach* i.e. a mournfull shout, they goe straight to the corps & there mourne bitterlie & cryes deeperatlie, oome of them will rent their linnen, hair & faces . . .'

Letter from James Garden to John Aubrey, 1692, Wiltshire Archaeological and Natural History Society MS

This is a season to be philosophical about matters of health and beauty

'An ague at fall of leaf is always of long continuance – or else short and fatal.'
Book of Iago ab Dewi, Welsh, fourteenth century

'Of Head affections and, firstly, of the Hair's falling off. Which is caused by an undue relaxing of the pores and by dispersion of the primary matters whence the hair has its growth; which being once totally dispersed, there is for the hair no more remedy.'

Medical tract, Irish, fifteenth century, B.L. Harleian 546

On this day in 1921, John Boyd Dunlop, Scottish inventor of the pneumatic rubber tyre, died

'The Celtic chariot was as small as its Egyptian predecessor; the step-up from ground to floor is only 1 ft. 10½ in. and that floor is only 3 ft. square. Its astonishing manoeuvrability, attested in contemporary record, is thus rendered possible. Its speed in roadless country depended on the remarkable technique of the Celtic wheelwright; the Llyn Cerrig finds enable us to add a rider that it depended also on the Celtic blacksmith. The tires were shrunk on as they are today and, what is more, are nail-less.

A detail of craft technique: "When I was a boy in Berkshire," an old-age pensioner remarked, "umbrella handles were bent by pushing the straight rods into a muck heap for from 24 to 48 hours when they bent very easily but needed to be tied across and left to set at least 8 and preferably 12 weeks." Rightly or wrongly, I like to think of the ashen bars, adzed for our Llyn Cerrig wheels, being thus prepared in the common midden of the settlement, half-farm, half-workshop, where the Celtic wright of the first century BC carried on his skilled, serviceable, and delightful trade.'

Sir Cyril Fox, *The Antiquaries Journal*, 1947

Scorpions should marry as soon as they can

In Scorpio it is advantageous to arrange marriages and to take a wife; they that shall be born are likely to live; he who takes to his bed shall be healed quickly, and his backbone suffers most.

Apostle: Peter

Ruler: Cronus

Medieval Irish Zodiac, Basle Library

For pain in the back

'Bleed from the back of the foot near the great toe, and fillet the limb, having bathed it in warm water, and the patient will surely get well.'

Meddygon Myddfai, Welsh, thirteenth century

Cornwall's largest fair is held on this day at Summercourt

Billy Treglase, a local balladeer, penned this advice for ladies:

'All the women of Summercourt Fair,
I'll give 'ee advice, then you can beware.
If your men do drink too much beer or gin,
You must scat [knock] 'em down with a rolling pin.
So, women, I hope you'll follow this plan,
If you should be plagued with a drunken man.'
Dean and Shaw, *The Folklore of Cornwall*

Reed month

Reckoned a tree by Irish poets, from which the swift-flying arrow shafts were made, and cut at this time of the year.

The festival of Dervilla of Erris in Mayo

This sixth-century saint is said to have put her eyes out because an unwanted suitor said they were the most attractive thing about her.

'Her waist is taper,
None is completer
Like the tuneful nine or the lambs at play;
And her two eyes shinin'
Like rowlin diamonds,
And her breath as sweet as the flowers in May.'
Irish ballad

' "I could put the eye of the cat in your lap in place of your eye," said the doctor to the young doorkeeper of Tara.
"I should like that as well," said the young man.
But this turned out to be a convenience and an inconvenience for him, for when he wished to sleep the eye would start at the squeaking of mice the flying of birds, and the motion of rushes: and when he wished to watch a host or assembly, then it was surely in deep repose and sleep with him.'
The Fate of the Children of Tuirenn, Irish tale, edited by T. P. Cross and C. H. Slover, 1936

October

Birth of Dylan Marlais Thomas in 1914, only son and younger child of David John Thomas, English master at Swansea Grammar School

The eloquence of the Welsh is legendary, and the land of Taliesin may also claim as a son one who sought, found and impressed the fabulous Prester John.

'Unto a rich pavilion he's directed
By men of state, where he is well attended
With all that's rich, and to his rest commended.
Some few days spent, and time for audience got,
When Prester John in royal state was set:
Jones, studying how t'express his eloquence
In some strange language which might pose the Prince,
Now trouls him forth a full mouthed Welsh oration
Boldly delivered as became his nation.
The plot proved right, for not one word of sense
Could be pick'd from it, which vexed the learned Prince.
His learned linguists are called in to hear,
Who might as well have stopped each other's ear
For aught they understood, and all protest
It was the very language of the Beast.'

David Lloyd (1597–1663), *The Legend of Captain Jones*

A hurling match

'"A thing happened to myself, Stevie, last autumn, coming on winter, and I never told it to a living soul and you are the first person now I ever told it to. I disremember if it was October or November. It was October because it was before I came up here to join the matriculation class."

Stephen had turned his smiling eyes towards his friend's face, flattered by his confidence and won over to sympathy by the speaker's simple accent.

"I was away all that day from my own place over in Buttevant at a hurling match between Croke's Own Boys and the Fearless Thurles and by God, Stevie, that was the hard fight. My first cousin, Fonsy Davin, was stripped to his buff that day minding cool for the Limericks but he was up with the forwards half the time and shouting like mad. I will never forget that day. One of the Crokes made a woeful swipe at him one time with his caman and I declare to God he was within an aim's ace of getting it at the right side of his temple. Oh, honest to God, if the crook of it caught him that time he was done for."'

James Joyce, *A Portrait of the Artist as a Young Man*, 1916

James Boswell, the Scottish biographer and diarist, was born this day in 1740

'At the same time, I could not help thinking that Mr Johnson showed a want of taste in laughing at the wild grandeur of nature, which to a mind undebauched by art conveys the most pleasing, awful, sublime ideas. Have I not experienced the full force of this when gazing at thee, O Arthur's Seat, thou venerable mountain! whether in the severity of winter thy brow has been covered with snow or in mist; or in the gentle mildness of summer the evening sun has shone upon thy verdant sides diversified with rugged moss-clad rocks and rendered religious by the ancient Chapel of St Anthony. Beloved hill, the admiration of my youth! Thy noble image shall ever fill my mind! Let me travel over the whole earth, I shall still remember thee; and when I return to my native country, while I live I will visit thee with affection and reverence!'

James Boswell, *London Journal*, 1762–3

Bees, chafers (restricted humming, tenuous buzz); barnacle geese, brent geese, shortly before Samhain (music of a dark wild one).

Anon, 'King and Hermit', ninth century, translated by Gerard Murphy

'And the learned say that the price of a chafer's leg of any kind of property was not left in the large central royal pavilion of the fort, except the cauldron that was about the demon's head.'

The Vision of Mac Conglinne, Irish, fourteenth century, edited by Kuno Meyer, 1892

Richard Brinsley Sheridan, dramatist, theatrical entrepreneur and politician, was born in Dublin in 1751

'When he was a boy at Harrow, under Doctor Sumner, an uncle Chamberlayne looked after his money accounts, and enforced upon him, considering his father's circumstances, the necessity of strict economy. He was not to compete for an archery prize, because competition involved the cost of an archer's costume. But inasmuch as, at the same time, he had a Greek oration to deliver in the character of

a military commander, he took upon himself to order of his tailor a general officer's uniform. When his astonished uncle produced the tailor's bill and expostulated, the boy replied that the speech was military, and that he could not have spoken a word of it if he had not looked like a soldier. That boy was father to the man.'

Sheridan died in great poverty in 1816.

October

November Eve: Hallowe'en

The crops should be in and the fruit collected, the cattle brought down from their summer pasture. Light a bonfire: mischief is abroad this night. This is the night when the dead leave their graves and may appear among the living. They may be bidden in the name of the devil to reveal the fate of the questioner. Stranger magic is possible on this night:

'By certain incantations, the dead can be made to appear and answer questions; but for this purpose blood must be sprinkled on the dead body when it rises; for it is said the spirits love blood. The colour excites them and gives for the time the power and semblance of life.'

Lady Wilde, *Ancient Legends, Mystic Charms and Superstitions of Ireland*, 1888

Discover the name of your future spouse

'Winnow a wecht of nothing, and ask what passes behind you the answer to your question, or wash a garment in a running brook, then hang it on a thorn bush and wait to see the apparition of the lover who will come to turn it.'

Scottish superstition

On All Hallows Eve a vicious and terrifying apparition – a cross between mule, a bullock and a big black pig, the Pooka – is liable to be met at night.

NOVEMBER

summer's end

Breton: *Mis Du* (black month)   Cornish: *Mis Du*
Irish: *Samhain* (summer's end)   Manx: *Sauin*
Scottish: *ceud mhios a' gheamhraidh*   Welsh: *Tachwedd* (remnant)

November

1
Samhain, 'summer's end' is the beginning of the Celtic year

'The old Welsh year, like the Celtic year generally, began on the first of November (*Calan Gaeaf*), and the importance attaching to that day has not yet quite disappeared. This is the old New Year's Day which Celtic tradition as a whole favours.'

Revd John Fisher, *The Welsh Calendar*, 1895

Winter's Day: death and fertility
Iron Age communities slaughtered their cattle, except for a few beasts kept through the winter to breed, at this festival of the division of summer and winter.

'Winter's Day, rough is the weather
unlike early summer;
there is no diviner but God.'

Welsh, early twelfth century

2
The Day of All Souls

'The Land of the Dead is at the western extremity of Great Britain to which the people of Armorica had to ferry the souls of the dead, impelled by unseen prompters to go in the middle of the night and board strange ships, their gunwales close to the water so heavy is their cargo. Breton folklore holds that the boats left from Baie de Dépassés in south-western Brittany.'

Procopius, *Gothic Wars*, sixth century

The Christian feast of All Souls dates from the ninth century AD, established by an abbot of the monastery of Cluny to give comfort to those suffering in Purgatory. During the Reformation, the authorities, disturbed by the pagan elements of the festival, removed it from the Church calendar. Not until 1928 was the day restored. Houses were cleaned, fires stoked, and a candle for each member of the family who had died was left to burn in an empty room until midnight. At the end of the nineteenth century, in parts of North Wales, it was still customary for small children to go out 'souling' – collecting little offerings of food for the returning souls.

Feast day of Saint Nuada, an anchorite, of whom nothing is known

But his name is that of a Celtic god, Nuadha (Irish), Nudd or Lludd (Welsh), whose temple at Lydney in Gloucestershire near the River Severn is a healing sanctuary of the fourth or fifth centuries AD with baths and cubicles for patients.

The connection with healing is a strong one: Nuadha, king of the Tuatha de Danann was maimed in the First Battle of Magh Tuiredh (in the Year of the World 3303) and had his arm replaced with a silver one, made by Dian Cecht the Leech, physician god of the immortals.

And as a watery god he may have had a hand in the great flood of 1099, on this day, when 'as well in Scotland as England, the Sea broke over the Banks of many Rivers, drowning divers Towns'.

Britain's Remembrancer, 1676

Each parish had its patron saint

In Ireland, Wales, Brittany and the Highlands of Scotland there was scarcely a parish that did not keep the annual feast – the pattern or pardon – of their local saint at the holy well or shrine associated with their name. These gatherings were also local holidays, and fairs.

'There were certain fairs held in Anglesey known as *Mabsantau* (patron saints), devoted entirely to hiring and pleasure. They are still held at Bodedern and Trefdraeth at the beginning of May and November.'

Royal Commission on Labour, Wales, 1893

'Though the trade is now better distributed throughout the year the important fairs still fall at the turning points of the pastoral year, at the beginnings of May and November. These two points are also still the Irish gale-days, when rents fall due.'

E. Estyn Evans, *Irish Folk Ways*, 1957

The Coligny Calendar

'1897, in Coligny, France, 126 fragments of a very ancient bronze calendar were found. Restoration found that the language of the Calendar was strikingly similar to Old Irish. This Celtic find gives us the earliest use of the "borrowing days" – the first day of Canlos, which may roughly be taken to have been May, has opposite it Edrini, which is the genitive of the name of the previous month: in other words, the first of May is a day of April, and enjoys April weather. The Calendar also starts its year in November (Quitios), to which Celtic folklore unanimously points as the calends of winter and the beginning of the year.'

John Rhys, 'Celtae and Galli', *British Academy Proceedings*, 1905–6

Leave stalks on garden plants for the frosts to attack and the roots will be protected

'He stole away once more to the house of Oth, over crisp grass one morning; and the old witch knew he had gone but did not call him back, for she had no spell to curb the love of roving in man, whether it came early or late. And she would not hold back his limbs when his heart was gone to the woods, for it is ever the way with witches with any two things to care for the more mysterious of the two. So the boy came alone to the house of Oth, through his garden where dead flowers hung on brown stalks, and the petals turned to slime if he fingered them, for November was come and the frosts were abroad all night.'

Lord Dunsany, *The King of Elfland's Daughter*, 1924

Visit a holy well with a grave complaint

'There is considerable evidence to show that the first Sunday of each quarter in the Celtic year was the proper day for the suppliant to pay his vows at the holy well when the healing virtue of their waters was at its utmost potency. The first Sundays of November, February, May and August were the chief days of resort to the healing fountains (owing to inclemency of the seasons, February and November are far less popular).'

J. M. McPherson, *Primitive Beliefs in the North East of Scotland*, 1929

'If the spirit of the well were outraged, it might cease to give forth healing virtue. A farmer from Letterewe, whose favourite dog had gone mad, brought it to the holy well at Innis Maree to get a drink of the healing waters. The dog was cured, but the offended spirit departed from the well forever. It ceased to heal.'

Gordon Cumming, *In the Hebrides*, 1883

Nine nights and a night unreckoned from Hallowe'en to the Eve of the Feast of St Martin

Sheep were brought down from the mountains, and servants who had been hired for harvest were discharged.

'Between Hallowmass and Christmass, when the people laid in their winter provisions, about twenty-four beeves were killed in a week; the best not exceeding sixteen or twenty stone. A man who had bought a shilling's worth of beef, or an ounce of tea, would have concealed it from his neighbours like murder.'

John Brand, *A Statistical Account of Scotland*, 1793

In Merioneth, at the time of the slaughter, neighbours gathered in each other's houses in turn to eat meat: the word *ciga* means meat-eating, and the poor were given broth and leftovers.

November

Long dark evenings signal company: sit by your neighbour's fire and set the world to rights

'Come then! and while the slow icicle hangs
at the stiff thatch, and winter's frosty pangs
Benumb the year, blithe (as of old) let us
'Midst noise and war, of peace and mirth discuss.
Vex at the times' ridiculous misery –
An age that hath fooled itself, and will
(Spite of thy teeth and mine) persist so still?
Let's sit then at this fire, and while we steal
A revel in the town let others seal,
Purchase or cheat, and who can, let them pay.'

'An Invitation to Brecknock', Henry Vaughan (1621–1695)

The pith of the soft rush (Latin, *Juncus effusus*; Irish, *Geataire*), provided the wick for rush-lights

'Like everything else about her lately, her hair was sluggish and hung heavily down, but after a few minutes under the quickening strokes of the brush, it lightened and lifted, and soon it flew about her face like the spray above a weir. It had always been the same, even when she was a child. She had only to suffer the first painful drag of the bristles when her mother would cry out, "Look! Look! That's electricity!" and a blue spark would shine for an instant like a star in the grey depths of the mirror.

That was all they knew of electricity in those dim-lit days when valleys of shadow lay deep between one piece of furniture and another. Was it because rooms were so badly lit then that they saw it so often, that little blue star?'

Mary Lavin, *In the Middle of the Fields*, 1964

Hollandtide Eve, Old Hallow Tide, when it is the custom, particularly in country districts, for boys to go from house to house shouting out these words:

'Hop-tu-Na – This is old Hollandtide night:
Trolla-la – The moon shines fair and bright.
Hop-tu-na – I went to the well,
Trolla-la – And drank my fill;
Hop-tu-na – On my way back
Trolla-la – I met a witch-cat;
Hop-tu-na – The cat began to grin
Trolla-la – And I began to run.
Hop-tu-na – Where did you run to?
Trolla-la – I ran to Scotland.
Hop-tu-na – What were they doing there?
Trolla-la – Baking bannocks and roasting collops.
Hop-tu-na – Trolla-la
If you are going to give us anything, give it to us soon
Or we'll be away by the light of the moon – Hop-tu-na!'
William Harrison, *Mona Miscellany*, c. 1870

This day is also St Martin's Day, when no wheel is allowed to turn.

Samhain, Old Style

Laa'l Souney in the Isle of Man. The season or month was called *Yn Tuayn*, because anciently it was the first day of the year. Today was the general day for letting lands, payment of rents, menservants taking their places for the year, and commencement of the winter half-year.

'Bonfires were formerly kindled at this time, as well as at Midsummer. When the embers had partially burned out, those who assembled were accustomed to cast them about in various directions, or sometimes at each other, with no slight danger to those who were not skilful in parrying or escaping from the burning brands. The high streets or market squares of towns and villages, or fair-greens and cross-roads in the country places, were usually selected for kindling this Samhain pile.'
Leinster lore, *Lageniensis*, 1870

November

The Battle of Sheriffmuir, fought on this day in 1715, signalled the exile of the Old Pretender

Donald M'Queen was servant to the Baron Seaton of Fyvie, who fled to France after the 1715 rebellion, and died there. Donald returned with one of his master's best horses, and 'cast the glamour' over his mistress, Lizzie Menzie, the Lady of Fyvie, by an unusual means.

'O wae wat worth you, Donald M'Queen,
Alas! that ever I saw thee:
The first love token ye gae me
Was the tempting cheese o' Fyvie.
O woe be to the tempting cheese,
The tempting cheese o' Fyvie
Gart me forsake my ain gudeman
And follow a footman laddie.'

Scottish ballad

To the modern mind there is nothing romantic about cheese. Yet it has been known to prove effectual as a charm in winning the heart even of one not of the mortal race. The hereditary Physicians of Myddfai are sprung from the otherworldly Lake Maiden and the young Welsh farmer who won her by dropping a large cheese and a loaf of bread into the waters.

Ageless philosophy

'In son or wife take no delight, neither for aught that is in this world make moan: all that will be as God shall please, nor will be in any other wise than that.'

James Beton, a member of the Macbheatha family, who were hereditary physicians in Islay and Mull in the sixteenth century

'Time is the tick of a clock. Good and evil are two peas in the one pod. My wife's face is the same forever. I want to play with the children, and yet I do not want to. Your conversation with me, brother, is like the droning of a bee in a dark cell. The pine trees take root and die. It's all bosh. Goodbye.'

James Stephens, *The Crock of Gold*, 1912, reviewed this day in 1912 by Walter de la Mare

The feast day of Saint Malo, dragon-quieter and friend of little birds

Malo was a Welshman, and sixth-century bishop of the town on the Emerald Coast in France.

While travelling with Saint Brendan he met a sea-serpent which ate three boys before the eyes of the blessed crew. Saint Malo raised his staff aloft and made the sign of the cross over the dragon, who with a lengthy hissing, ceased to be harmful.

One day when Saint Malo was pruning his vines – for as a follower of Saint Paul, he believed that he should supply his own needs with his own hands – he found that a wren had laid her eggs in the cloak he had laid aside. Knowing that God has a special care for the birds and beasts he let his cloak lie, and until the eggs were hatched no drop of rain fell upon it.

Cut hazel twigs

'Now is the time to cut long hazel twigs to season over winter, ready for forming the skeletons of the Spring-built curraghs.'
J. Hornell, *British Coracles and Irish Curraghs*, 1938

The hazel was included among the seven most highly-prized trees in ancient Irish law: the rods were used for wattle walls of houses and fences, and the nuts were an important food from the time of earliest man.

Fionn Mac Cumhal as a boy acquired the wisdom of the Salmon of Knowledge who had himself acquired it by eating the nuts of the nine hazel trees that grow beside the well at the bottom of the sea.

The nuts are also useful for discovering the fidelity of a Welsh sweetheart by a means dating at least from the fourteenth century. Rival suitors took a handful of hazelnuts, *cnau mewn llaw*, 'nuts in hand', and whoever had the even number of nuts had the faithful lover.

Recipe for Welsh rarebit: the tempting cheese of Fishguard?

Stir 4 oz. of sharp and tasty grated cheese, 1 oz. butter and 3 tablespoons of milk or ale in a heavy pan over a low heat until they are creamy. Add pepper, salt and 1 teaspoon of hot mustard, and bring to just below boiling point. Place two slices of toasted bread in a heatproof dish, pour the cheese mixture over them and put the dish under a hot grill until browned.

'The Welch are said to be so remarkably fond of cheese, that in cases of difficulty their midwives apply a piece of toasted cheese to the janua vitae to attract and entice the young Taffy, who on smelling it makes the most vigorous efforts to come forth.'

Francis Grose, *A Classical Dictionary of the Vulgar Tongue, c.* 1800

'Burning the water' took place in the autumn when the fish were very 'red' and almost inedible

he fish are discovered by means of torches, or fire-grates, filled with blazing fragments of tar-barrels which shed a strong though partial light upon the water.

'On the present occasion, the principal party were embarked in a crazy boat upon a part of the river that was enlarged and deepened by the restraints of a mill-weir, while others, like the ancient Bacchanals in their gambols, ran along the banks, brandishing their torches and spears, and pursuing the salmon, some of which endeavoured to escape up the stream, while others, shrouding themselves under roots of trees, fragments of stones, and large rocks, attempted to conceal themselves from the researches of the fishermen.'

Sir Walter Scott, *Guy Mannering,* 1814

Earache is a common ailment at this time of the year

'Put a limpet on the fire and remove when the juice bubbles. When cool enough pour the juice in the affected ear and stop the ear with a bit of wool that still has the oil in it.'

Old Cures from South Uist

Or go to 'the sacred cave beyond Kessock Ferry, near the point of Kilmur, Ross-shire, known as the Dripping Cave of Craig-a-Chowie. Water drips from the roof, and even in modern times these drops have been regarded as a complete cure for deafness and earache. The patient lies down on the floor of the cave and lets the water fall first in one ear and then the other.'

J. M. McPherson, *Primitive Beliefs in the North East of Scotland*, 1929

The soil of a cave-floor is often believed to have curative powers.

The Tuatha de Danaan, when they were defeated as rulers of Ireland, became the Sidh, living under hills and lakes. Their powers are especially strong on Fridays.

Nor hare, nor leveret, nor coney

Old Mary said, 'God Almighty likes to see the hounds following the hares and routing the fox out of his burrows because that is according to his nature.'
'I wouldn't care for the coursing. I agree all hunting and coursing is horrible, though what old Mary from Gort says is half true.'

Jack B. Yeats to Lady Gregory thanking her for the gift of a hare, November 1921

'Friend, with regard to this same hare
Am I to hope, or to despair?
By punctual post the letter came,
With Powell's hand, and
        Powell's name:
Yet there appeared, for love
        nor money,
Nor hare, nor leveret, nor
        coney.'

Christopher Smart (1722–1771)
to the Revd Mr Powell, who
had promised the author a
hare, and failed to deliver.

November

Potatoes are harvested in November

Except for odd ploughing or digging work which had to be done before the hard frosts began, work on the land was finished until February, and attention could be turned to marriage-making and merriment.

In the northern counties of Ireland 'champ' is a traditional and delicious dish
Scrub two pounds of potatoes and boil them in their skins. Chop some spring onions and boil them in milk until they are tender. Drain, peel and mash the potatoes with the milk from the onions. Lastly mix the onions into the mashed potatoes and serve with butter.

'Potatoes are the seaman's greatest curse; there are only three places in the world where they are worth taking on board: Ireland, Argentina and Tristan da Cunha.'
Conor O'Brien, *Across Three Oceans*, 1927

St Cecilia's Day – patroness of music and musicians

Irish harps were said to have 'three strains', or styles: *Geanntraighe*, for laughter, dance and merriment; *Gollraighe*, for tears, sorrow and death; and *Suantraighe*, music to induce sleep.

The old Welsh way of life
'Then came the singing to the harp. Everyone was well-versed in the art, and there was no danger at all of its intricacies being bungled.'
O. W. Jones (1828–1870)

'Then there was that grand old man with a big voice, Bobby Gale, the basso profundo of the choir who, having a decided genius for composition, would occasionally bring his latest inspirations to be criticized. In one of these laudable attempts a full half – the better half, had been bodily cribbed. This the dear old man with delightful naiveté called "a remarkable coincidence", a phrase which thenceforth became proverbial among the Vicarage boys.'
W. H. Gill, 'Manx Miniatures', *Mannin*, 1914

Bringing up baby

In Sagittarius they that shall be born shall suffer danger to their youth; he who takes to his bed is healed slowly.
Apostle: Paul
Medieval Irish Zodiac, Basle Library

Cormac, the grandson of Conn of the Hundred Battles, was stolen as a newborn baby by a she-wolf, and nurtured with her own cubs. He brought his wolf-brothers with him when he returned to claim his father's throne. His death is said to have been caused by a salmon bone sticking in his throat.

The medieval Irish are said to have taken wolves for 'gossips' (i.e. godfathers and godmothers), and the Brehon laws show that they tamed and made pets of them as well as of cranes, hawks, foxes and deer.

S. H. O'Grady, *Silva Gadelica*, 1892

Whisky *go leor* – enough

On this day in 1993 the last fourteen bottles of Scotch whisky salvaged from the 1941 wreck of the *SS Politician*, the inspiration for Compton Mackenzie's book *Whisky Galore*, were sold at auction for £11,462.

'Courtship is unknown in Glenmornan. When a young man takes it in his head to marry, he goes out in company with a friend and a bottle of whiskey and looks for a woman. If one refuses, the young man looks for another and another until the bottle of whiskey is consumed. The friend talks to the girl's father and lays great stress upon the merits of the would-be husband, who meanwhile pleads his suit with the girl. Sometimes a young man empties a dozen bottles of whiskey before he can persuade a woman to marry him.'
Donegal author Patrick MacGill, *Children of the Dead End*, 1914

Carolan, the blind harper, composer of such songs as 'Receipt for Drinking', died in 1738 holding a bowl of whisky he had not the strength to drink. He murmured that it was hard 'that two such friends should part, at least without kissing'.

November

Laa'l Catharina: the feast day of St Catherine, martyred for preferring to remain a spinster

'Despondently she lay reclined
Her arms around this log entwined
Love tales she told to force applause
Her lips opposed to his lank jaws.
She oft on him had pressed and fawned
And he as oft had coughed and yawned
It was all in vain to raise his steel
By elbow aid long nail or heel
Or yet the rug to pluck in play
From off his rusty musty clay.'

Brian Merriman (*c.* 1747–1805), 'The Midnight Court'

Elder month

'Elder that hath tough bark, tree that in truth hurts sore: him that furnishes horses to the armies from the sidh burn so that he be charred.'

'Death of Fergus', Irish, early sixteenth century, B.L. Egerton MS 1782

'At Toome Island there is the ruin of an ancient church, where the dead walk on November Eve. It is a solemn and sacred place, and nothing is allowed to be taken from it; neither stone nor branch of the shadowing trees, for fear of angering the spirits. One day three men who were on the island cut down some branches of an elder-tree that grew there to repair a private still, and carried them off in their boat; but when just close to the shore a violent gust of wind upset the boat, and the men were drowned. The wood, however, floated back to the island, and a cross was made of it which was erected on the beach, to commemorate the fate of the doomed men.'

Lady Wilde, *Ancient Legends of Ireland*, 1888

Laa'l Machold geuraoh, St Maughold's winter feast in the Isle of Man

27

The boar, the national emblem of Gaul, was used as a crest on Celtic helmets

Associated with the underworld, with the oak whose fruits he ate, and with strength and courage, the boar was venerated in the darkness of winter.

'And they roused that combative boar, so that all the hounds and packs and warriors of the *fian* saw him. The description of that huge boar were enough to cause mortal terror, for he was blue-black, with rough bristles ... grey, horrible, without ears, without a tail, without testicles, and his teeth standing out long and horrid outside his big head. Then from every direction a neck and neck race of hounds and warriors began towards him. And that ... of a redmouthed beast wrought a slaughter of hounds and men of the *fian* on that spot.'

The Chase of Sid na mBan Finn and the Death of Finn,
edited by Kuno Meyer 1910

28

Season of mists

'Avaunt, thou filthy, clammy thing,
Of sorry rain the source and spring!
Moist blanket dripping misery down,
Loathed alike by land and town!
Thou watery monster, wan to see
Intruding 'twixt the sun and me.'

Attributed to Daffyd Ap Gwilym, fourteenth century, translated by George Borrow

Nora (taking the stocking with the money from her pocket, and putting it on the table): 'I do be thinking in the long nights it was a big fool I was that time, Michael Dara; for what good is a bit of a farm with cows on it, and sheep on the back hills, when you do be sitting looking out from a door the like of that door, and seeing nothing but the mists rolling down the bog, and the mists again and they rolling up the bog, and hearing nothing but the wind crying out in the bits of broken trees were left from the great storm, and the streams roaring with the rain.'

J. M. Synge, *The Shadow of the Glen,* 1905

November

The beginning of Advent: the 'Shrovetide of the Lent of Winter'

St Adamnan's Vision of Hell: an eternity of cold and damp for those who had abused the Church and her possessions

'Great multitudes there are, standing in blackest mire up to their girdles. Short cowls of ice are on them. Without rest or intermission, through all time, their girdles are perpetually scorching them with alternate cold and heat. Demon hosts surround them, with fiery clubs in their hands, striking them over the head, though they struggle against them continually. These wretches all have their foreheads to the North, and a rough, sharp wind blowing full upon their foreheads, in addition to every other woe.'

St Adamnan, *Second Vision*, Leabhar Brecc, Irish, fourteenth century

Vision of William of Stranton at Saint Patrick's Purgatory, Pettigo, County Donegal

' . . . y saw fendes [fiends] with grete strength pullyng and teryng adown the pilars of þe brigge, and the bisshop sodaynly fallyng into þe water and his meyne with him. And in the fallyng my thowght y saw a bright angell takyng away the myter and the cros fro þe bisshop and vaneshid away.'

Fifteenth century, B.L. Add. 34, 193

St Andrew's Day, National Day of Scotland

'Scotts – As to humour . . . I never knew a fool of that Nation.'

John Aubrey, 1684–6, Royal Society MS

'It is especially dangerous to be out late on the last night of November, for it is the closing scene of the revels – the last night when the dead have leave to dance on the hill with the fairies, and after that they must all go back to their graves and lie in the chill, cold earth, without music and wine till the next November comes around.'

Lady Wilde, *Ancient Legends of Ireland*, 1888

'And, vow! Tam saw an unco sight!
Warlocks and witches in a dance!
Nae cotillon brent new frae France,
Bur hornpipes, jigs, strathspeys, and
    reels,
Put life and mettle in their heels.
A winnock-bunker in the east,
There sat auld Nick, in shape o' beast –
a touzie tyke, black, grim, and large!
To gie them music was his charge:
He screw'd the pipes and gart them
    skirl,
Till roof and rafter a' did dirl.
Coffins stood round like open presses,
That shaw'd the dead in their last
    dresses;
And by some devilish cantraip sleight
Each in its cauld hand held a light,
by which heroic Tam was able
To note upon the haly table
A murderer's banes in gibbet-airns.'

Robert Burns (1759–1796), *Tam O'Shanter*

[Shanter is a farm near Kirkoswald, in the southern division of Ayrshire.]

DECEMBER

month of black storms

Breton: *kerzu, kerdu, keverdu*   Cornish: *Cevardhu*
Irish: *nollaig* (Christmas)   Manx: *Mee ny Nollick*
Scottish: *meadhonach a' gheamhraidh* (midwinter)   Welsh: *Rhagfyr*

December

1 Winter in Arran, in the Firth of Clyde

' . . . and during winter the men make their herring nets while the women are employed in spinning their linen and woollen flax.'

Thomas Pennant, *A Tour in Scotland and Voyage to the Hebrides*, 1772

Súith na Móna: peat soot, if boiled in a muslin bag for a hour or so, will make a dye that turns wool a dark yellow-brown or auburn shade.

Recipes for the Dyeing of Wool

'Arran of the many stags,
The sea strikes on its shoulder,
Isle where companies are fed,
Ridge on which blue spears are reddened.

Skittish deer are on her peaks,
Delicious berries on her manes
Cool water in her rivers
Mast upon her dun oaks,

Greyhounds are there and beagles,
Blackberries and sloes of the dark blackthorn,
Her dwellings close about the woods,
Deer scattered about her oak-woods.'

'The Colloquy of the Old Men', Irish, thirteenth century, translated by Kuno Meyer

2 Mungo Park, surgeon, botanist and explorer, was born in 1771 at Fowlshiels, Selkirkshire, seventh of thirteen children of a tenant of the Duke of Buccleuch

On 2 December 1795, under the auspices of the Association for the Promotion of Discovery, he set out with six servants, a horse, two mules, an umbrella, compass, sextant, thermometer, fowling piece and pistols to find the source of the River Niger. Of his experiences he wrote: 'Whatever difference there is between the Negro and the European in the conformation of the nose and the colour of the skin, there is none in the genuine sympathies and characteristic feelings of our common nature.' He died, drowned in the Niger, on a second expedition in 1806.

Chambers and Thomson, *Eminent Scotsmen*, 1870

Make *poitín* for the Christmas season now

Barley and malt are the preferred ingredients, but, at a pinch, potatoes can be used; they certainly were in the eighteenth century.

The potatoes must be exposed to frost over several nights, then cut into slices and left in water to steep for ten days, stirring occasionally. Strain off the water and add to it yeast and treacle. This is the 'wash'. Allow to ferment, and then distil without boiling.

'Throw a glassful on the fire: if the flame is white – that's *poitín*.'

Donegal

Plain and homely food of the country

'The country people of North Britain [Scotland] live chiefly on oatmeal, and milk, cheese, butter, and some garden-stuff, with now and then a pickled herring, by way of delicacy; but flesh-meat they seldom or never taste; nor any kind of strong liquor, except twopenny, at times of uncommon festivity.'

Tobias Smollett, *The Expedition of Humphry Clinker*, 1771

'It is said that the devil will not come to Cornwall for fear of being put into a pie: the Cornish people make pies of almost anything eatable, as squab-pie, starey-gazey-pie, herby-pie or muggetty-pie.'

Francis Grose, *Provincial Glossary*, 1811

December

5

A cure for chilblains

'When you go to bed at night put your hands or feet in very hot water, then dry thoroughly with an old linen cloth, patting so that the linen takes back all the moisture from the pores. Put them right up to the fire for a good while. Then make an oatmeal poultice, just like porridge without salt, leaving it on until morning. Then make another poultice and put it on without washing the feet. But at night begin with the very hot water as you did before and continue for a week and it will cure them.'

Old Cures from South Uist

6

The Winter Pardon of Saint Barbe, patron saint of explosives and artillerymen, takes place at Le Faouët on the first Sunday in December. She is also invoked during storms

'Strange, how silence makes one notice things! When the eleven o'clock hooter sounded a hush fell on the whole of the pit; on trucks, crowbars, wedges, and hammers; and in the three-minutes interval before the blasting-hooter everyone hurried to the shelter-cabin. Everyone, that is, except my father, who lingered by my side until I sent him packing. I watched him moving slowly away, pausing for a moment to gaze at the flock of crows hovering above the pit; they, too, knew that it was firing-time. I heard the crunch of his boots on fragments of slate, and then it ceased for a moment as he halted to watch Richard Roberts – "Dick Mysterious", as we called him – bending over the fuse on the other side of the pit.'

T. Rowland Hughes (1903–1949), translated by Richard C. Ruck

7 Guard your pretty daughters against theft by the fairies

'The fairy chiefs greatly desire a handsome mortal wife . . . the children of such
unions grow up beautiful and clever, but they are also wild, reckless and
extravagant. They are known at once by the beauty of their eyes and hair, and
they have a magic fascination that no one can resist, and also a fairy gift of music
and song.'

Lady Wilde, *Ancient Legends of Ireland,* 1888

'Young people should be *conducted,* but that's where they're all astray,
There were none o' this loiterin' home from fairs in Father M'Carthy's day;
'Twas he would ha' had their lives for less, so he would then, who but he!
Your mother he called "the flower o' Layde", an' none minds that but me.
And she had the song of a song-thrush, but you have the laugh of a jay,
Oh, she was a rose in December, but you are a frost in May!'

Moira O'Neill, *More Songs of the Glens of Antrim,* 1911

8 Time to bring livestock inside: protect them from the cold wet weather

'The rain that comes in the Black Month
Enters the horse up to its liver
So fatal is December rain.'

Breton proverb

'As in the rest of Brittany the livestock use the same entrances as the people, and
they are not far from sleeping together.'

M. Duboisson-Abenay, seventeenth-century visitor to Brittany

'We once saw, near Josselin, a man drive into his cabin a cow, a horse, followed by a
pig, and, afterwards entering himself, he shut the door.'

Mrs Charles Stothard, *A Tour of . . . Brittany,* 1820

Ensure that you get your heart's desire for Christmas

'Golden butter on a new made dish, such as Mary set before Christ. This is to be given in the presence of a mill, of a stream, and a tree; the lover saying softly – "O woman, loved by me, mayest thou give me thy heart, thy soul and body, Amen." This will effect love.'

Lady Wilde, *Ancient Legends of Ireland*, 1888

'The kepie stone or needle in the Dee near Dinnet had the power of making the childless wife a joyful mother, if she passed through its magic circle. The hole is about eighteen inches in diameter.'

J. M. McPherson, *Primitive Beliefs in the North-East of Scotland*, 1929

'There is one hour in every day when any wish you make will be granted, but it is not known when it is.'

Irish saying

Alban Arthan: the winter equinox Old Style

(Given in some Welsh MSS as the beginning of the year)

'He lived in a low room over a coach-house; and that was not by any means at the back of the North Wind, as his mother very well knew. For one side of the room was built only of boards, and the boards were so old that you might run a penknife through into the north wind. And then let them settle between them which was the sharper!'

George Macdonald, *At the Back of the North Wind*, 1871

The author was born this day in 1824, in a tiny house in Aberdeenshire, where he and his five brothers slept in box-beds with sliding doors to keep out the North Wind.

'Welkin's wind, way unhindered,
Big blusterer passing by,
A harsh-voiced man of marvels,
World-bold, without foot or wing,
How strange that sent from heaven's
Pantry with never a foot,
Now you race so swiftly
Over the hillside above.'

Dafydd ap Gwilym (*fl.* 1280)

Llywelyn ap Gruffydd, last native Prince of Wales fell in battle this day in 1282, at Cilmery, near Builth

'Since the death of Llywelyn, my human reason fails me, chill is the heart in my breast for dread, and sportiveness withers like the dry brush-wood.'

Gruffudd ab yr Ynad Coch, 'Elegy', 1282

'A red-speared man, a man grief-stricken like Priam
A fine man as king over the proudest army,
A man whose fame will spread easily – most generous his outlay –
as far as the sun travels on his furthest course.'

'Bleddyn Fardd', Welsh, thirteenth century

Festival of Saint Corentin, fifth-century Bishop of Quimper

Saint Corentin dwelt in a hermitage in the parish of Plou-Vodiern, at the foot of Mont Saint Côme where there was a little spring of water in which lived a miraculous fish. Each day Corentin cut off a piece of its flesh and returned it to the spring, where it made itself whole again before the next meal.

'One day he received a visit from two eminent saints and he was in despair. He had flour, and could give them pancakes for dinner, but pancakes, before it was understood how to season them with sugar, nutmeg and lemon, were thought very insipid. He went to the fountain to look at his fish. If he broiled for his visitors the entire fish he would have killed his golden goose. But he found the spring full of plump eels! He cooked them for dinner in light wine, and his visitors left, licking their lips, and glorifying God for having given them so dainty a meal.'

Revd Sabine Baring-Gould, *Lives of the Saints*, 1877

December

The auguries of a dirty winter's night

13

'"Indeed, Martin," said my father, "there is a wind from the north and an inhospitable appearance on the Beanna Bana: there will be rain before morning and a dirty stormy night before us that would put trembling on you if you were in your bed itself. And look how bad that omen is, Martin, that the ducks are amongst the nettles. Disappointment and great piteousness on the world tonight, the bad-thing and the sea-cat will be on the march together with the darkness, and if it's true for me there won't be one piece of good fortune before the both of us ever."

"Indeed, Michelangelo," said Martin O'Banasa, "not little the saying the amount of your saying, and if it's true for you, no lie you have in it but the truth itself."'

Myles na gCopaleen, *An Béal Bocht*, 1941

The yew is the Celtic tree of death

14

In Brittany it is believed that the roots of the graveyard yew seek out the mouths of those buried there.

'Patriarch of long-lasting woods is the yew, sacred to feasts as is well known: of him now build ye dark-red vats of goodly size.'

'Death of Fergus', Irish, early sixteenth century, B.L. Egerton MS 1782

The Irish yew, *Taxus baccata 'fastigiata'* (the 'steep' or 'sharpened' yew) is a compact and columnar variety grown from a 'freak' tree discovered on a Fermanagh mountainside in 1767 by the head gardener of the first Earl of Enniskillen. All examples since have been grown from the specimen still standing in the park at Florencecourt.

Almost all of the yew is poisonous, all except the red aril, or berry. But the stone within the aril is poisonous too. The main symptom of yew poisoning is sudden death.

The famous Tay Whale

'Twas in the month of December, and in the year 1883,
That a monster whale came to Dundee,
Resolved for a few days to sport and to play,
And devour the small fishes in the silvery Tay.

Oh! it was a most fearful and beautiful sight,
To see it lashing the water with its tail all its might,
And making the water ascend like a shower of hail,
With one lash of its ugly and mighty tail.'
William McGonagall, *Poetic Gems*, 1890

'Hit is a fisch of this grete see, the greteste that there is,
Jascom he is i-cleped, and fondeth nigt and dai
To putte his tail in his mouth, ac for gretnisse he ne mai.'
'The Metrical Life of St Brendan', fourteenth century, B.L., Harleian MS 2277

The sea-girt Celts

'Bitter is the wind tonight,
It tosses the ocean's white hair:
To-night I fear not the fierce warriors of Norway
Coursing on the Irish Sea.'
Medieval Irish, translated by Kuno Meyer, 1913

The seashore bore a harvest of seaweed, thrown up during the great winter storms, and gathered for manure. It was also burned to make kelp, in the eighteenth century a valuable commodity, used to make glass, soap, bleach and iodine; it might pay the rent and buy some of life's luxuries – tobacco and spirits; packed around meat, fish and cheese, kelp was also a preservative.

Charles Peel, a Fellow of the Zoological Society was a frequent visitor to the Western Isles in the 1880s. He remembered the ocean's gifts of one year to the coast of North Uist: cases of champagne, West Indian beans, tins of Vaseline, a turtle and a lamp, still workable. The people of the island greatly enjoyed the Vaseline, which they spread on bread and ate with delight.

**It is reckoned that all Breton wines but Muscadet should be drunk with
caution – and preferably only drunk while leaning against a supporting wall**

' "Ye put me in mind of yer father, when he'd taste a drop long ago. I saw him
smashin' every plate on the dresser long ago, an' leoga, he was the man that slaved
hard to keep a house goin'. There's breeds of people an' drink drives them fair daft,"
she warned.

"There's breeds of drink that fair drives any man daft," he
defended.'

Peadar O'Donnell, *Islanders*, 1928

**The feast of Saint Maighnenn, who gave his name to the hospital of
Kilmainham in Dublin**

'A prophecy of Bishop Magnenn's was: that a time should come when there should
be daughters flippant and tart, devoid of obedience to their mothers; when they of
low estate should make much murmuring, and seniors lack reverent cherishing;
when there should be impious laymen and prelates both, perverted wicked judges,
disrespect to elders; soil barren of fruits, weather deranged and intemperate
seasons; women given up to witchcraft, churches unfrequented, deceitful hearts and
perfidy on the increase; a time when God's commandments should be violated, and
Doomsday's tokens occur every year.'

S. H. O'Grady, *Silva Gadelica*, 1892

19

***Mabinogion* hero Lleu Llaw Gyffes changes his name with the seasons: in midwinter he is the Eagle of Nant y Llew**

'There is a remarkable eagle which lives in the mountains of Snowdonia. Every Thursday it perches on a particular stone, hoping to satiate its hunger with the bodies of dead men, for on that day it thinks war will break out. The stone on which it takes its stand has a hole pierced nearly through it, for it is there that the eagle cleans and sharpens its beak. An eagle is said to know the place where it can find its prey, but not the time. A raven knows the time, but not the place.'

Gerald of Wales, *Journey through Wales*, late twelfth century

This may be one of the pair of eagles which, as Geoffrey of Monmouth says, guarded the grave of King Arthur on Snowdon.

20

At the end of the eighteenth century, with the increase in sheep-farming, it became customary to employ a fox-hunter and to pass the Christmas holidays in hunting the fox

'I little thought that the result would be that three weeks later I should find myself in a railway carriage at an early hour of a December morning, in company with Flurry Knox and four or five of his clan, journeying towards an unknown town, named Drumcurran, with an appropriate number of horses in boxes behind us and a van full of hounds in front. Mr Knox's hounds were on their way, by invitation, to have a day in the country of their neighbours, the Curranhilty Harriers, and with amazing fatuity I had allowed myself to be cajoled into joining the party. A northerly shower was striking in long spikes on the glass of the window, the atmosphere of the carriage was blue with tobacco smoke, and my feet, in a pair of new blucher boots, had sunk into a species of Arctic sleep.'

Somerville and Ross, 'In the Curranhilty Country', *Some Experiences of an Irish R. M.*, 1899

December

Computing the Solstice

'The length of time that the sun spends in each sign is 30 days 10 hours; and the time that he takes to run his course is 18 score days and ten minutes, with 5 days 7 hours 10 minutes added. Whence is produced the Solstice: called "the Station of the Sun" and taking place when he ceases from his progression away whether from the length or from the shortness of the day ... i.e. from the twelfth day before Christmas ... [and] from the 22nd day before St John's. The which if one understands accurately, the computi are no ways opposed thereto: since in every 6 score years the Solstice, on account of the minutes that we mentioned above, gains a day. In proof of which at Christ's birth the lengthening began with Christmas day ...'

Irish, 1589, B.L. Cotton Appendix LI

Standing stones and stone circles are aligned on the sun, the moon and the stars and served their creators as a kind of stone calendar.The great burial mound of Newgrange, for example, is oriented on the winter Solstice, as is Stonehenge in Wiltshire.

In Scottish Gaelic, *Dùgan* means the darkness of a loch, and *Dùgan a' gheamhraidh* the darkest time in winter.

On this day in 1989, Samuel Beckett, playwright and novelist, who was born in Foxrock, Dublin in 1906, died. His first novel, published in 1932, was entitled *Dream of Fair to Middling Women*

'When a companion exclaimed that the beauty of the day made one feel good to be alive, Beckett replied: "Well, I wouldn't go so far as that."'

Enoch Brater, *Why Beckett*, 1989

Little Mary of the Fair Hair

'Her likeness is as the sun of the summer
Honey grows behind her on the track of her feet in the mountain
Seven weeks after November day.'

Douglas Hyde, *Love Songs of Connaught*, 1893

' ... to us, as to the Ancient Irish, the half-said thing is dearest.'

Kuno Meyer, *Ancient Irish Poetry*, 1911

Capricorn

In Capricorn those who shall be born are likely to live; he who takes to his bed is quickly healed and his knees mostly suffer: he who is in chains is quickly loosed.
Apostle: Matthew
Ruler: Hyperion

Medieval Irish Zodiac, Basle Library

'There are three tedious complaints: disease of the knee joint; disease of the substance of a rib; and phthysis; for when purulent matter has formed in one of these, it is not known when it will get well.'

Medical triad by Taliesin, Welsh, sixth century

Hunting the wren

On the Isle of Man wren hunting was said to be the occupation of Christmas Eve, until it was time to begin Christmas. A crowd would go out and hunt the tiny bird, kill any unfortunate specimen found, lay her on a bier with great solemnity and sing dirges over her in the Manx language.

'In Warleggan, Cornwall, on Christmas Eve it was customary for some of the household to put in the fire and the rest to take a jar of cider, a bottle, and a gun to the orchard and put a small bough into the bottle. They then said, "Here's to thee, old apple tree! Hats full, sacks full, great bushel bags full! Hurrah!" and fired off the gun.'

T. Quiller Couch, *Western Antiquary*, 1883

December

A Triad of Hospitality

Y Nadolig (Welsh); *Notlaic* (Old Irish); *Nollick* (Manx); *Nadelic* (Cornish); *Nedelic* (Breton); *Natalicium* (Latin): birthday.

Three things prohibited to a chief: an ale-house without cheese; a crowd of people without mirthful noise; a host without hounds.

Guaire, King of Connaught, had never been satirized for lack of generosity, and Senchán decided to bring the bardic company to his house. Out of sympathy for his intended host, however, he brought only two thirds of his following.

'Guaire received them and told them to ask for anything they wished for. It was a difficult situation because each had to be served alone, occupy a separate bed, and always some one of them had a peculiar or difficult wish, which the king had to gratify or suffer satire.'

The Burdensome Company of Guaire, Irish, thirteenth century, edited by James Carney

'In the cider-making valley of Avillion it is said that when the moon is full on Christmas night, there will be a year of apples.'

Breton proverb

The Druids' bird

n St Stephen's (or Boxing) Day the wren was suspended in a garland of flowers, ribbons and evergreens. A procession carried the 'king of all birds' (as the Druids called it) from house to house, soliciting contributions, and giving a feather for luck: these were considered an effective charm against shipwreck.

The *dreain*, or wren's feathers, were considered a preservative against witchcraft; this word comes from *druai dryw*, the Druid's bird.

The wren is called in Latin, *regulus*; French, *reytelet*; Welsh, *bren* (king); Teutonic, *Koning Vogel* (king-bird); and in Dutch, *Konije* (little king).

Eadar a' da la Nodlag – between Christmas Day and New Year's Day the
mummers took to the streets

'There was St George and St Denis and St Patrick in their buffe coats, and the
Turke was there likewise and Oliver Cromwell and a Doctor, and an old woman
who made rare sport, till Belsibub came in with a frying pan upon his shoulder and
a great flail in his hand thrashing about him on friends and foes, and at last running
away with the bold usurper, Cromwell, whom he tweaked by his gilded nose – and
there came a little Devil with a broom to gather up the money that was thrown to
the Mummers for the sport. It is an ancient pastime, they tell me, of the Citizens.'
'A visitor to Cork', 1685, T.C.D., MS 1206

'. . . what a world of money he had gathered at the gentlemen's houses when he
acted Beelzebub in the Christmas mummers.'
Sir William Wilde, *Irish Popular Superstitions*, 1852

Sir James Matthew Barrie, son of a hand-loom weaver of Forfarshire wrote the story
of the boy who never grew up for his sons: on this day in 1904 his play *Peter Pan*
was first performed, and has been revived at Christmas ever since.

Innocents' Day

'Innocents' Day, or Childermas, called in Medieval Welsh literature *Gwyl y fil
feibion*, the Festival of the Thousand Sons.'
Revd John Fisher, *The Welsh Calendar*, 1895

'It is very unlucky to wash [clothes] on Innocents' day, washing is still not done at
St Austell on the 28th of December: which is about the only saint's day we keep.'
Joseph Hammond, *A Cornish Parish: being an account of St Austell*, 1897

'Now from within the harbour
we will launch out into the deep
and see what luck of fish there
God shall send us which (so
you talk not of hares or such
uncouth things, for that proves
as ominous to the fisherman as
the beginning a voyage on the
day when Childermas Day fell
doth to the mariner) may
succeed very profitable.'
Richard Carew, *Survey of Cornwall*, 1602

December

The mistletoe, or golden bough

Called golden because of the yellow colour of the leaves and stalks when kept. Bretons hung great bunches of it above their doors at the winter Solstice; by midsummer it was the colour of heaven's fire.

The Celts worshipped the oak, the strongest of the trees, as the great god: mistletoe which grows on the oak is believed to be the hiding place of the life of the host. The Druids cut the parasite with gold, not iron, and ensured that it never touched the ground, thereby losing its healing properties. A specific for epilepsy, tumours, sterility and witchcraft.

The oak grove, in Irish, is *doire*, often 'derry' in place names.

'This is why I love Derry
it is so calm and bright
for it is all full of white angels
from one end to another.'

Attributed to St Colum Cille, Irish, fifteenth century, translated by Gerard Murphy

On this day in 1691 Robert Boyle, youngest son of the Earl of Clanricarde, eminent philanthropist and chemist, inventor of Boyle's Law, enthusiastic propagator of the Gospels, died

The Reverend Robert Kirk, incumbent first of Balquidder and then of Aberfoyle, a 'gentle Jacobite' and author of the learned treatise *The Secret Commonwealth: of Elves, faunes and fairies*, first published, by Sir Walter Scott, in 1815, became deeply concerned about the lack of translations of the Scriptures into Gaelic, and sought the help of Robert Boyle. 'Boyle's Bible', in archaic Irish type was distributed in Scotland in 1688.

Hogmanay

At this season in France it was the Druidical custom, as remarked by Selden, on going out to cut the mistletoe, for the young fellows about New Year's tide in every village to give the wish of good fortune at the inhabitants' doors, saying 'Au guy l'anneuf' which is a corruption of the old formula, *Hoguinanno*.

In the Isle of Man it was the popular belief that the Hogmen, or hilmen, or elves, removed their quarters, and a general 'flitting' took place, and were to be met with in all directions, hence the wish to propitiate them. Thus 'Hogmen-aye' means 'Elves for ever!'

'The stone at Quoybune in Birsay, every Hogmanay night, when the clock strikes twelve, marches down to the Loch of Boardhouse and dips its head in the water. It is not safe to watch this occurrence.'

J. M. McPherson, *Primitive Beliefs in the North-East of Scotland*, 1929

Sources of Illustrations

Arabic numerals refer to days of the month, Roman to the months:

J. A. Atkinson 31/V; Basel: Öffentliche Bibliothek der Universität 21/I, 20/II, 22/III, 21/IV, 22/V, 22/VI, 27/VII, 24/VIII, 23/IX, 24/X, 23/XI, 23/XII; J. D. Batten 4/I, 1/II, 3/II, 16/VII, 10/IX; T. Bewick 10/III, 3/VI, 25/VIII, 14/IX, 5/XII; Birmingham: Reference Library, Stone Collection 30/VIII; P. Bridgewater 21/II; H. K. Browne 7/XII; E. Calvert 28/IX; Cambridge: Fitzwilliam Museum frontis., 3/II, 22/VII; Cardiff: The National Museum of Wales 22/VIII; Peter Clayton 21/XII; Cologne: Rheinisches Bildarchiv Dombibliothek 14/VI, 11/VII, 17/VIII; J. Constable 20/IX; Copenhagen: Ny Carlsberg Glyptotek 2/I, Nationalmuseet 23/X; G. Cruikshank 19/II; R. Dadd 27/VI; L. Dickinson 13/XI; G. Doré 12/IV, 16/XII; Dublin: Abbey Theatre 18/IV, Archives of Municipal Corporation of Dublin 30/VII, Irish Tourist Board 31/I, 6/VIII, National Library of Ireland 1/IV, 1/VI, 11/IX, National Museum of Ireland 2/VI, 23/VIII, 3/XI, The Board of Trinity College title page, February frontis., 29/II, March frontis., April frontis., May frontis., 24/V, June frontis., 3/VII, 24/VII, 13/VIII, October frontis., 18/XI; H. J. Ford 25 & 26/IV; A. Fussel 9/III; P. Gauguin 3/X; A.-L. Girodet de Roucy-Trioson 17/II; Glasgow: Burrell Collection 3/X; M. Gonne 6/I, 2/II, 8/II, 6/V, 17/V, 3/VIII, 18/VIII, 18/XI, 26/XII; E. Griset 9/I, 5/II, 19/V, 15/X; © Sonia Halliday Photographs 17/III; J. D. Harding 8/IV; T. Higham 7/VII; W. Hinches 17/IV; H. Inman 4/III; J. Joly 1/IV, 1/VI; J. Kay 2/IX; H. Lachmann 16/X; E. T. Leeds 23/I, 24/I; W. Lewis 28/III; L. Litchie 10/V; London: By permission of the British Library 29/III, 5/IV, 11/V, July frontis., August frontis., 19/VIII, September frontis., 21/X, November frontis., 15/XI, December frontis., Copyright British Museum 10/IV, 30/IV, 14/V, 31/VII, 15/VIII, 17/IX, 1/X, 30/X, Christie's 12/XI, Mary Evans Picture Library 18/I, 25/I, 13/III, 15/III, 23/IV, 28/IV, 2/V, 28/V, 15/VI, 13/VII, 2/VIII, 14/X, 25/XI, Images Colour Library 10/IX, Public Record Office 6/IV, © Tate Gallery 27/VI, Victoria & Albert Museum 20/IX, 25/X; Lyons: Musée de la Civilisation Gallo Romaine 5/XI; D. Maclise 26/VI; Malmaison: Musée de Malmaison 17/II; Kenneth Markham 23/VII; P. Metcalf 26/III; J. E. Millais frontis.; O. Montelius 19/IV; George Mott half-title, January frontis., 26/III, 18/VII, 2/XI; Newcastle upon Tyne: Museum of Antiquities 25/II, 10/XI; Sister C. O'Lynch 18/VII; Oxford: The Bodleian Library 24/VI, 4/IX, 10/X; Paris: Bibliothèque Nationale 26/II, 29/III, 5/X, 18/X, 7/XI, 19/XII, Jean-Loup Charmet 7/I 31/XII, Musée Carnavalet 13/IV; J. Piper 13/II; A. Rackham, courtesy of the Arthur Rackham family 7/III; G. Raverat 5/V, 11/VIII; courtesy R. Rosenberg 1/I, 3/I, 13/II, 19/II, 24/II, 27/II, 1/III, 5/III, 9/III, 10/III, 11/III, 14/III, 24/III, 3/IV, 8/IV, 10/IV, 30/IV, 14/V, 29/V, 31/V, 7/VII, 15/VIII, 1/IX, 12/X, 14/IX, 16/IX, 20/IX, 28/IX, 1/X, 30/X, 8/XI, 3/XII, 5/XII, 7/XII, 13/XII, 28/XII, 29/XII; D. G. Rossetti 14/III, 22/VII; St Gall: Stiftsbibliothek 9/VI, 22/XI; St Germain-en-Laye: Musée des Antiquités Nationales 27/XI; O. Sheppard 6/VIII; Benjamin Stone 30/VIII; W. Stukeley 24/VI, 4/IX; after W. Stukeley 21/XII; J. M. Synge 1/VII;

Eileen Tweedy 6/II, 17/IV, 3/VI, 30/VII, 25/X; W. Ward 24/III; Washington, D.C.: The Naval Historical Foundation 6/IX; D. Wilkie 5/III; J. B. Yeats 14/IV, 25/X.

Books and manuscripts

Adamnan *Vita Sancti Columbae* (9th century) 9/VI; Anon. *World of Wonders* (*c.* 1880) 26/I; *Bateman's Tragedy; History of Unfortunate Love* (1720) 5/VI; T. Bewick *History of British Birds* (1797–1804) 6/II, 24/II, 9/VII, 26/IX, 29/XII; *Book of Common Prayer* (1695) 3/V, 9/VII; The Book of Durrow, March frontis., April frontis., May frontis., June frontis., 3/VII, October frontis.; The Book of Kells, title page, February frontis., 29/II, 24/IV, 24/VII, 13/VIII, 18/XI; W. M. Bottrell *Hearthside Stones in the West of England* (1870) 31/VIII; N. Bourne *The Wonderful Battel of Starelings* (1622) 12/I; E. W. Brayley *Popular Pastimes* (1815) 1/I; Canterbury Psalter of St Augustine 1/III; Caradoc of Llancarvan, *History of Wales*, 1774 17/I; G. Chaucer *Canterbury Tales* (*c.* 1483) 10/II; F. Cornford *Mountains and Molehills* (1934) 11/VIII; J. Dennys *The Secrets of Angling* (1652) 12/XII; The Echternach Gospels 29/III, 7/XI, 19/XII; Erasmus, *In Praise of Folly* 29/I; J. Evelyn *Silva* (1776) 29/V; *The Excursions Through Ireland* (1819) 7/VII; *The Famous History of the Lancashire Witches* (1870) 31/III; J. Gerard *Herball* (1636) 19/VI; *The Glasgow Mercury*, 13–20 July 1786 11/X; T. Hale *Compleat Body of Husbandry* (1756) 9/VIII; *Handbook of the Shetland Islands, Kirkwell* (1878) 3/XII; Harman *Caveat* (1567) 19/VIII; *Hortus sanitatis*, 1491 3/IV; *The Illustrated London News*, 12 August 1843 27/VII, 10 January 1846 9/X, 12 August 1843 17/XII; M. Jackson *The Pictorial Press* (1885) 13/XII; A. Kircher *Arca Noë* (1675) 29/VI; *Letters from a Gentleman in the North of Scotland to his Friend in London* (1754) 28/XII; The Lindisfarne Gospels 29/III, 5/IV, July frontis., August frontis., September frontis., 21/X, November frontis., 15/XI, December frontis.; J. Logan *The Clans of the Scottish Highlands* (1845) 19/III, (1847) 13/XI; Luttrell Psalter 14/V, 15/VIII, 17/IX, 1/X, 30/X; P. A. Mattioli *Commentarii* (1565) 16/VIII; J. Meydenbach *Hortus sanitatis* (1491) 23/VII; T. Moore *Irish Melodies* (1866) 26/VI; J. Oxenham *A True Relation of an Apparition* (1641) 13/I; J. Parkinson *Paradisi in sole Paradisus terrestris* (1629) 2/III, *Theatrum botanicum* (1640) 11/III; Peacham *Minerva Britannica* 15/I; T. Pennant *British Zoology* (1812) 8/III, *Tour in Scotland* (1772) 20/I; G. de la Perrière *Le Théâtre des bons engines* (1536) 25/VII; C. de Plancy *Dictionnaire infernal* (1863) 31/X; Plautius *Nora typis transacta navigatio* (1621) 16/V; J. Romilly Allen *Early Christian Symbolism in Great Britain and Ireland* (1887) 29/IX; J. Sherer *Rural Life Described and Illustrated* (1869) 20/XI; Sir R. Sibbalds *Miscellanea quaedam eruclitae antiquitatis* (1710) 2/X; A. Tennyson *Idylls of the King* (1868) 12/IV, 16/XII; E. Topsell *The History of Four-footed Beasts* (1607) 17/VI; Vespasian Psalter 11/V; I. Walton *The Compleat Angler* (1931) 7/III; J. D. C. Wickham *Records by Spade and Terrier* (1918) 16/II; J. B. Yeats *The Aran Islands* (1907) 21/IX.